Hans Urs von Balthasar

My Work: In Retrospect

HANS URS VON BALTHASAR

My Work:
In Retrospect

COMMUNIO BOOKS
IGNATIUS PRESS

Title of the German original:
Mein Werk—Durchblicke
© 1990 Johannes Verlag
Einsiedeln, Freiburg

Cover by Roxanne Mei Lum

ISBN 0-89870-435-9
Library of Congress catalogue number 92-74535
Printed in the United States of America

CONTENTS

FOREWORD

Hans Urs von Balthasar made detailed statements about his work on five occasions, mostly on the birthdays that marked the end of a decade of his life: as a young author, in his desire "to lift out of the jumble of history the four or five figures who, taken together, represent for me the constellation of my idea and my mission"; as publisher and writer, "out of concern for the reader" and in order to equip this reader with a guide to the quickly spreading thicket of books written and published by him. Then, in the midst of the transformations and new beginnings connected with the Council, he wrote *In Retrospect* for himself and for all his readers, inside and outside the Church, about what had been given and what had been done and what was still required and planned. Finally, in a kind of pause, as one already looking toward the close of his life, he gave once again an account of what had been achieved and what could no longer be achieved, in a clear shift of emphasis away from his "authorship" in favor of pastoral work in the communities he had founded. A few weeks before his death, he attempted once more a "glimpse through my thinking", a simple and clear text that is only a few pages long. In the meantime, he had also been able to complete his trilogy.

This present volume is a helpful guide to his many-layered work.

Cornelia Capol

7

I

AN INTRODUCTION:
HANS URS VON BALTHASAR

1945

One of the great blessings of God is that no one sees himself as he really is; even when he looks at himself in a mirror, he sees himself in a reversed mirror image. But others, who discover much in him that he does not know, in turn know little of what he himself knows about himself. And thus ultimately—if we prescind from the omniscience of God—the least unreliable measure of a man remains his work. "You will know them by their fruits", and yet, since these fruits can be deceptive, you will not "judge them" by these. Thus, all that a writer can do is to send his books to the front, if he is to give information about himself—even if he can only laugh at these advocates, who correspond so little to what he fundamentally would have wanted to say. He is the ungrateful man who, like the Spartan of old, exposes the newborn behind the nearest bush, already planning (like some Don Giovanni of the spirit) to bring something new and better-shaped into the world.

"Nothing is so delightful as the ability to lift out of the jumble of history the four or five figures who, taken together, represent for me the constellation of my idea and my mission": so we read in a certain book called

Translated by Fr. Brian McNeil, C.R.V.

Weizenkorn (The grain of wheat).[1] Well, just as I was once constrained as a boy to plough my way through the entire undergrowth of Romantic music from Mendelssohn via Strauss to Mahler and Schönberg, before finally I was allowed to see rising behind these the eternal stars of Bach and Mozart—and, for a long time now, these two have taken the place of all others a hundred times over —so, too, I had to clear my path through the jungle of modern literature, in Vienna, Berlin, Zürich and other places, until at last the kindly hand of God took hold of me (as once he took hold of Habakkuk along with his bowl [see Dan 14:33−39]) and chose me for a true life. But here, once again, everything was different; one had to begin at the beginning and eat one's way through endless stretches of spiritual literature, like eating one's way through a pastry mountain to get to the land of milk and honey (and the mountain was perhaps as dry as it was sweet), until gradually, in the course of theological studies, the true encounters came. Many of the ancient stars had retained undiminished their powerful light: Plato, Hölderlin, above all Goethe and Hegel; likewise, I would never again forget some of the words and gestures of Nietzsche. But now brighter stars began to shine alongside these; and, for having caught sight of the true ones, I must thank my undeserved friendship with the greatest spirit whom I have been permitted to meet, Erich Przywara. His first book appeared in 1936, encouraged by Josef Pieper and his Institute for Popular Education in Dortmund: excerpts from Augustine's Commentary on the Psalms, a work that, although completely unknown

---

[1] *Das Weizenkorn* (Lucerne: Räber, 1944; 3d ed., Einsiedeln: Johannes Verlag, 1989), 34.

to German readers, belongs to his most profound works, along with the sermons and the treatise on the Trinity. Another friend, Henri de Lubac, drew my attention to the Alexandrians, and so I discovered Origen and recognized in astonishment that he was the most sovereign spirit of the first centuries, who has set his mark for good or ill on the totality of Christian theology; a selection of his texts, to which I could give no other title than *Origenes, Geist and Feuer (Origen: Spirit and Fire)*,[2] was intended to allow his inner image to appear afresh in all its bold sublimity, and this book, which has received little recognition, seems to me even today the weightiest of all I have published.

A wider panorama opened up from this point, backward to the glorious Irenaeus,[3] to Clement and especially to the lyrical and sensitive Gregory of Nyssa, who offered a smaller range than the Alexandrian giant but, nevertheless, the greatest joy.[4] And so the obscure and steep Max-

---

[2] *Origenes, Geist und Feuer. Ein Aufbau aus seinen Werken* (Salzburg: Otto Müller, 1938; revised and expanded ed., 1953). English translation: *Origen: Spirit and Fire: A Thematic Anthology of His Writings* (Washington, D.C.: Catholic University of America Press, 1984). Cf. also: *Parole et mystère chez Origène* (Paris: Éditions du Cerf, 1957).

[3] *Irenäus, Geduld des Reifens. Die christliche Antwort auf den gnostischen Mythos des 2. Jahrhunderts*, Klosterberg Collection (Basel: Schwabe, 1943). 2d improved ed., Sigillum Collection 6 (Einsiedeln: Johannes Verlag, 1956). New ed.: *Irenäus, Gott in Fleisch und Blut. Ein Durchblick in Texten*, Christliche Meister Collection 11, with revised introduction (Einsiedeln: Johannes Verlag, 1981). English translation: *The Scandal of the Incarnation: Irenaeus against the Heresies*, selected and with an introduction by Hans Urs von Balthasar (San Francisco: Ignatius Press, 1990).

[4] Gregory of Nyssa, *Der versiegelte Quell. Auslegung des Hohen Liedes*, abbreviated translation with introduction (Salzburg: Otto Müller, 1939); 3d ed., Sigillum Collection 3 (Einsiedeln: Johannes Verlag,

imus the Confessor offered a concluding synthesis of the patristic world of the spirit (*Kosmische Liturgie* [Cosmic liturgy],[5] *Gnostische Centurien* [Gnostic centuries]).[6] Finally, there were gleanings: in the course of my readings, the lost scriptural commentaries of Evagrius Ponticus and the missing first commentary on Dionysius by John of Scythopolis fell into my hands: both of these opened up extremely significant vistas in terms of the history of ideas.[7] Alongside these ran the study of Thomas Aquinas, whose genuine vitality disclosed itself to me in his less central writings, for which I would dearly love, *Deo favente*, to publish an overall interpretation. But, first of all, the new horizons had to serve to bring to a conclusion the plan I had conceived as an inquisitive student of German literature but had not been able to carry out, thanks to my lack of training in the history of ideas. Thus it was that those three strange tomes with the equally strange title appeared: *Apokalypse der deutschen Seele. Studien zu einer Lehre von letzten Haltungen* (Apocalypse of the German soul. Toward a theory of fundamental orientations),[8] which attempted (to the insuperable horror of all

---

1954). New ed., revised according to the critical edition, Christliche Meister Collection 23. Cf. also: *Présence et pensée. Essai sur la philosophie religieuse de Grégoire de Nysse* (Paris: Beauchesne, 1942; 2d ed., 1988).

[5] *Kosmische Liturgie. Höhe und Krise des griechischen Weltbildes bei Maximus Confessor* (Freiburg: Herder, 1941); 2d, completely revised ed., with two further studies: *Die gnostischen Centurien des Maximus Confessor* and *Das Scholienwerk des Johannes von Scythopolis* (Einsiedeln: Johannes Verlag, 1961; 3d ed., 1988).

[6] In: *Herders Theologische Studien* 61 (Freiburg, 1941). See n. 5.

[7] *Das Scholienwerk des Johannes von Scythopolis*. In: *Scholastik* 15:16–38.

[8] *Apokalypse der deutschen Seele. Studien zu einer Lehre von letzten Haltungen*, vol. 1: *Der deutsche Idealismus*; vol. 2: *Im Zeichen Nietzsches*; vol. 3:

right-thinking specialists) to present in a total Christian interpretation poetry, philosophy and theology from Lessing to the present day. I readily admit that even I find this giant child somewhat monstrous; I often ask myself, when I see it on the bookshelf, what its contents may be. Perhaps it contains too much—but much of it was written at that time with my heart's blood.

Everything, then, was running true to course, and it seemed that I, as collaborator of a periodical in Munich, was destined to become the perpetual student of the intellectual sciences. But the boots of the SS sounded ever more loudly from the nearby Ludwigstrasse, and no ear could escape the loudspeakers that were set up everywhere in the city. The area around the old Hofbräuhaus became eerie and terrible, and I was glad to be offered the position in Switzerland that transferred me to direct pastoral work. Fresh student life brought new life into unrealistic theoretical knowledge, and the little time that still remained at my disposal was now used for a looser form of publication. A publishing firm in Basel wanted a series of books that would preserve the cultural heritage of the West: Was there any reason to refuse such a rewarding task? My old love for the great Catholic poets of France awakened anew: Why not make them familiar to the German reader in worthier dress? Thus the translations of Paul Claudel's *Cinq grandes odes*,[9] *Soulier de*

Die Vergöttlichung des Todes (Salzburg: A. Pustet, 1937–1939). New ed. of vol. 1: *Prometheus. Studien zur Geschichte des deutschen Idealismus* (Heidelberg: F. H. Kerle, 1947).

[9] Paul Claudel, *Fünf grosse Oden* (Freiburg: Herder, 1939; 3d ed., Einsiedeln: Johannes Verlag, 1964). Cf. also *Gesammelte Werke*, vol. 1: *Lyrik* (Einsiedeln: Benziger; Heidelberg: F. H. Kerle, 1963).

satin,[10] *Le Chemin de la Croix*,[11] and *Poesies*[12] were made; Péguy's *Le Porche du mystère de la deuxième vertu*[13] was translated under the thunder of canons from nearby Alsace; the anthology *Frankreich erwacht* (France awakens) was a small victory celebration.[14] But the heritage of the great saints of the Church was not to be left behind in the meantime; in order to remedy the deplorable fact that we read the most beautiful documents of the Christian spirit, namely, the writings of the saints, only through the blurring veil of portraits, biographies and interpretations, the collection *Menschen der Kirche* (Men of the Church) was founded. I put at the head of this series a new selection from Augustine;[15] thanks to capable and faithful collaborators, it promises to develop into a living presentation of high ecclesial spirituality. Henri de Lubac deserved to have his beautiful work *Catholicisme* (*Catholicism*) translated into German,[16] for seldom has a

[10] Paul Claudel, *Der seidene Schuh* (Salzburg: Otto Müller, 1939; 11th ed., 1987).

[11] Paul Claudel, *Der Kreuzweg* (Lucerne: Stocker, 1943). From 1957, in: *Corona Benignitatis Anni Dei*, 3d ed. (Einsiedeln: Johannes Verlag, 1965). Cf. also *Gesammelte Werke*, vol. 1: *Lyrik*.

[12] Paul Claudel, *Gedichte*, Klosterberg Collection (Basel: Schwabe, 1942). 3d ed., Christ heute 3/1 (Einsiedeln: Johannes Verlag, 1953), under the title *Der Wanderer in der Flamme*). Cf. *Gesammelte Werke*, vol. 1: *Lyrik*.

[13] Charles Péguy, *Das Tor zum Geheimnis der Hoffnung* (Lucerne: Stocker, 1943; 2d revised ed., Einsiedeln: Johannes Verlag, 1980).

[14] *Frankreich erwacht* (Lucerne: Stocker, 1945).

[15] Augustine, *Das Antlitz der Kirche. Auswahl und Einleitung.* Menschen der Kirche in Zeugnis und Urkunde (Einsiedeln: Benziger, 1942; 2d ed., 1955).

[16] Henri de Lubac, *Katholizismus als Gemeinschaft* (Einsiedeln: Benziger, 1943); 2d ed. (Einsiedeln: Johannes Verlag, 1970) under the title: *Glauben aus der Liebe*.

book drawn so fully from the patrimony of the greatest Christian tradition.

But preservation and translation could not be the whole task. The tree of tradition must put forth new branches; why should the one who gives form to what has been handed down from the past never do anything more than express his own thought through other people's voices? For now it suddenly seems to him that he himself has not yet said anything. Modestly, therefore, he begins to bind into a bouquet a few truths that he himself is perhaps the first to grasp fully in their undeveloped power (*Das Weizenkorn*),[17] following these with a sequence of hymns to Christ in rhythmical prose[18] (not a "book about Christ", as the publisher wrote on the jacket). All this is scarcely more than a beginning: the greatest part still remains unsaid. How much in theology still needs to be given a new form, in order to lead today's man anew to the most vital dimension of God, of Christ, of the Church! How much remains to be done for the encounter of modern thought with patristic and scholastic thinking! Every time one opens the Bible, it seems to require interpretation anew! Few verses have remained more alive in my consciousness than the monologue of the goldsmith in Hofmannsthal's *Kleines Welttheater*, when he looks down from a high bridge into the strong and swiftly flowing waters; he thinks he sees the body of the night:

> Now she unwinds her limbs; and now they throng,
> Reel into wild and separate commotion.

[17] See n. 1.

[18] *Das Herz der Welt* (Zurich: Arche Verlag, 1945), 4th ed., with new foreword (Ostfildern: Schwabenverlag, 1988). English translation: *Heart of the World* (San Francisco: Ignatius Press, 1980).

A drunken urge possesses me: I long,
My fingers itch, to mould those images,

Yet there are far too many, and all true;
One rises up, the others melt away.
Never I'll hold that flux, until I learn
To isolate one shape and make it stay. . . .[19]

And yet, at the moment when everything that is formed
and delimited is isolated in the work, it no longer seems
to be living wholly out of the great life of God, and so
we give it back and return it to this infinite sea of truth,
grateful that we have been permitted at least for a moment to share in giving it a form, in obedience to a mission and a task, so that it may become a guiding image
for someone else, if God permits. "All is yours, but you
are Christ's": I would like to have these words set as the
motto over what I have done.

[19] Nun wirft sie auseinander ihre Glieder / Und für sich taumelt jedes
dieser wilden. / Mich überkommt ein ungeheurer Rausch, / Die Hände
beben, solches nachzubilden,

Nur ist es viel zu viel, und alles wahr: / Eins muss empor, die an-
deren zerfliessen. / Gebildet hab ich erst, wenn ichs vermocht, / Vom
grossen Schwall das eine abzuschliessen. . . .

Gedichte und Lyrische Dramen (Stockholm: Bermann-Fischer, 1946),
382. English translation taken from Hugo von Hofmannsthal, *Poems and
Plays*, bilingual edition, ed. Michael Hamburger (New York: Bollinger
Foundation, 1961), p 243.

II

A SHORT GUIDE TO MY BOOKS

1955

One who turns fifty and has written a great deal that is apparently very disparate may well have cause to reflect: not least out of concern for the reader, who is h⁀ "neighbor", for the most part an unknown person who comes into contact with the author when he reads something the author finished long before and bestows a new presence on something that lies far away in the past. Out of concern, therefore, to make things easier for him by indicating the connections and intentions—in the literary work, not at all in the work of his life, whose decisions lie somewhere else again, and at a deeper level. It is not possible to make a clean separation between these two; a book must reflect much of the meaning that the writer seeks to give his own existence, even if this meaning is rather often stamped on the book against the direct will and supposition of the author. The magnet that hangs over him follows incomprehensible laws as it shifts its position, and all the filings change their place and form a new pattern with a plan that does not lie in the filings themselves. Whoever has truly experienced this gives up the attempt to bring his literary work into harmony with his life; when he writes, he is ahead of himself in a dream of the totality in which he would like to give his fragments a sure home; then once more he limps along behind his own self, or even creeps backward and looks around,

Translated by Fr. Brian McNeil, C.R.V.

like Lot's wife, into a beloved image of the past, an image that entices all the more magically since it is already ablaze. . . . Who can keep up? I was touched early in my life by Schiller's insight that the past is not something firm and closed but can be shaped through the decisions of the present; this is the hope of one who drags along the ever heavier chains of his books. He inevitably remains for the public the man of his past works, whereas it is only with reluctance, indeed, with anxiety, that he himself touches one of these snakeskins that betray to him with certainty that he no longer stands at that point, that he has long since become another man. He was the man of this idea, as it rose fresh in him, but only half that, as he reduced it to the form of a book and wrote this book in impatience to be finished with it—but afterward? Perhaps one robs oneself of the last credit one possesses in the eyes of one's readers when one makes such confessions; but is it not better for me to come right out and confess that I am an impatient man for whom one thing is beyond question: namely, that the book that has just been finished contains (once again) nothing of what absolutely ought to have been said, shown and made perceptible? The next book will be the product of desperation over the last one. This bitter pill brings calm; it is the penance I gladly undertake for that one excessive drop of delight that lies in all writing. It is superfluous to say that this is why I do not wish to be tied down to any of those forms I have traced in monographs in the course of the years, no matter how dear most of these remain to me, no matter what mysterious constellations they form through their mutual relationships—constellations that can suddenly be overwhelmingly clear for the one who studies them with even a little more love and yet remain only arbitrary rigid lines in that endless sparkle of light that no eye will ever be able to shape into constellations: the community of saints.

Be that as it may, it may be accepted as an act of politeness if I attempt to come with a rough map of the terrain to help the reader who is confused by the multiplicity of the themes broached in my work. Most of the territory here is undeveloped and will remain so; it is not my intention to assemble the *disjecta membra* artificially so as to give the illusion of a totality (albeit a grandiose totality). But the map shows a few streets on which one can walk even today; more are indicated by dotted lines; this shows the location of houses that have already been built; and so I cannot avoid revealing a few sketches of what is planned—*salva profidentia!*, which usually directs everything in such a refreshingly different manner.

I cannot begin without pointing out that my own work is what it is only in unity with others. Let me mention only the two most important: the work of the one to whom I was so greatly indebted during the years of my theological studies and for a long time afterward that many of the chief themes in my work go back to things pointed out by him: Erich Przywara. Still more decisive is the link to the work (still mostly unpublished) of Adrienne von Speyr, which I have seen come into being since 1940 and which I am gradually editing for publication. It corresponds in themes and tone to those of my own books. Missions often interpenetrate each other in the community of the Church, so that, if one were to take from one person all that he has received from others, only a dry stem would remain. Even if nothing in my work were original (and that would not surprise me), there would still remain the passion to hand on what has been preserved to others (because it is unfamiliar to so many), together with the order to do this; for missions more than personal qualities are what individualize the Christian.

There are three distinct areas to which my questioning is directed: the revelation of the fullness of God in Jesus Christ—the Church as the fullness of Christ—the radiation of the Church into the world.

I

For John, the revelation of God in Christ is the Incarnation of the Word in this One, who is unique, loved and adored; Ignatius appears to me as the point in history where the encounter of man with the God who is the Word and has the word, who addresses, chooses and calls, has become inescapable. In my view, all that is decisive takes place in the spiritual space that lies between the two poles of John and Ignatius.

1. The maturing Christian who must choose his life is led by Ignatius to the personal encounter with Christ: into a contemplation of the concrete Gospel situation (*applicatio sensuum, compositio loci*: the application of the senses, the composition of the scene, and so forth), which is determined by the "call"—as the basic concept of the life of Jesus—and "choice"—as the central act of the encounter. Christ chooses and calls us; our choice of him is only the answer that obedience makes: "so that we may attain to perfection in whatever state or life that God our Lord places before us for our choice". Consequently, perfection is not an impersonal ethical-religious canon of rules but is the obedience of the person to the Lord in the focus of the Gospel that continues to take place. Thus I

endeavored to translate the *Exercises*[1] in such a way that the glowing fire of the personal *majus*, "still more"—the rhythm common to Ignatius and John—resounds in the word.[2] Love is ablaze with enthusiasm, love makes a choice, demands exclusiveness—this is the source of the "counsels of Christ"—so that, from this point outward, it may become universal as Christian love; love becomes "Holy Spirit" only when it knows first that it is bound by the inexorability of the fleshly "here and now", the constraint of "bread and wine". Thus the Exercises appear fresher and more relevant than ever; they have functioned far too little in these four hundred years as the charismatic kernel of a theology of revelation that could offer the unsurpassed answer to all the problems of our age that terrify Christians.[3] The beginning and the end of everything remain the adoring prostration before the One who says, "It is I, I with whom you are speaking"—and John is full of this. A series of books with points for meditation on Sacred Scripture should begin in autumn 1955, which might help toward this act. In the encounter with the word of Scripture, God the Word must be dis-

[1] Ignatius von Loyola, *Die Exerzitien* (Lucerne: Stocker, 1946; 10th ed., Freiburg: Johannes Verlag Einsiedeln, 1990).

[2] Commentaries on this would be both E. Przywara's *Deus semper major* (1938/1940) and the fundamental work of Adrienne von Speyr, *Johannes* (four volumes, 1948/1949), in which the entire course of events is expounded as love. English translation: *John*, vols. 1–4 (San Francisco: Ignatius Press, 1987–).

[3] I have often given lectures at conferences on the idea of the Exercises, their fundamental philosophical and dogmatic bases, about the encounter between the thought of Ignatius and modern thought in a theology of election. Naturally, what is most important takes place each time in the Exercises themselves, which one cannot "give" without oneself sharing in receiving them anew from their origin.

covered and experienced, verse for verse, as the infinite
Word who judges and redeems.[4] More and more, everything tends toward the indivisible act of hearing the word,
which is at the same time an act of prayer, of faith and of
obedience—but, unlike the Protestant understanding of
the word, this is an act of hearing in the Church of the
ministerial office and of tradition, the hearing of a Word
that is at one and the same time flesh and blood in the
sacrament and—in one's neighbor.

2. The God encountered in the flesh is also the man
chosen from eternity, in whom everything in heaven and
on earth is recapitulated, who redeems the world and ele-
vates his brothers to become children of the Father. What
Paul calls the great "mystery" is that action of God with
the world that through creation, revelation and redemption always remains history, action, drama and event and
has its center in the fullness of time, in the Incarnation.
The aphorisms *Das Weizenkorn* (The grain of wheat)[5] already had the intention of experiencing the world and life
in this way; still more clearly is this true of the thirteen
hymns to Christ of *Das Herz der Welt* (*Heart of the World*),[6]
in which I wished to give back to the idea of the Heart of
Jesus (which has so often degenerated into sentimental-
ity) its cosmic dimension and, even more than this, the
incalculable and ultimately trinitarian inner sphere of the
hypostatic union. The christocentric idea took on the-

---

[4] The numerous commentaries on Scripture by Adrienne von Speyr
published by Johannes Verlag already indicate the path.

[5] *Das Weizenkorn* (Lucerne: Räber, 1944; 3d ed., Einsiedeln: Johannes
Verlag, 1989).

[6] *Das Herz der Welt* (Zurich: Arche Verlag, 1945), 4th ed., with
new foreword (Ostfildern: Schwabenverlag, 1988). English translation: *Heart of the World* (San Francisco: Ignatius Press, 1979).

oretical formulation in *Karl Barth* (*The Theology of Karl Barth*)[7] and especially in the *Theologie der Geschichte* (*A Theology of History*),[8] which was written directly as a result of this book. What is involved here is the integration of the form of time as such into the process of revelation: Christ, as the one who obeys the Father and follows him, the one who awaits the "hour", subjects himself to the law of the time of creation and thus becomes the criterion for redeemed time and for all history. In the meantime, I have attempted a further step, which still needs careful meditation: to shed light on the connections between ontology and Christology. If Christ is the concrete first Idea of the creating God—not in the Scotist sense—and thereby the goal of the world, then it must be permissible to explore the depths of the proposition, "Once (and for all!) Being [*Sein*] was in 'Existence [*Dasein*]' ".[9]

---

[7] *Karl Barth. Darstellung und Deutung seiner Theologie* (Cologne and Olten: Hegner, 1951; 4th ed., Einsiedeln: Johannes Verlag, 1976). English translation: *The Theology of Karl Barth* (San Francisco: Ignatius Press, 1992).

[8] *Theologie der Geschichte* (Einsiedeln: Johannes Verlag, 1950; revised ed., 1959; 5th ed., 1985). English translation: *A Theology of History* (New York: Sheed and Ward, 1963).

[9] The same goal is sought in a number of unpublished studies of the *Distinctio realis* (the "ontological difference"), in which the attempt is made to go beyond the Thomism of the schools to develop a real-ontology (which would be phenomenological in Conrad-Martius' sense) of the fundamental relationship between *esse* and *essentia*: but since their nonidentity displays such diverse and, indeed, contrary aspects (which have their effects, beyond pure philosophy, in art, religion and intellectual history, too), it is only a dialectic (in the sense of the methodology practiced by Alois Dempf) that can bring them to a deeper mutual coordination. Ontology here stands united to anthropology and then discloses itself anew as theological-christological.

From such a central point, the question of the relation between Being and act, or the question of the event-
character of the *actus* (*essendi*), becomes newly acute. The
philosophical monograph *Wahrheit. Erstes Buch. Wahrheit
der Welt* (Truth. First book: Truth of the world),[10] which
aims to open up the philosophical access to the specifically Christian understanding of truth, shows that this
does not mean taking the side of any nominalism or ex-
istentialism. The theme of the second volume must be
God in Christ in the Church as truth. I wanted first of all
to present the unity of the theoretical, the ethical and the
aesthetic, of the aspects of nature and of person, of truth as
not-being-hidden [*Unverborgenheit*] (the Greek idea) and
as reliability and fidelity (the Hebrew idea), of the attitude of truth as justice and as love, as the opening of the
subject for the object, the unity of natural openness and
a free self-revelation of the subject, and accordingly the
mysterious character of all truth and the verbal character
of all manifestation of Being, the path from the appearing
to image and word, the unity of disclosure and conceal-
ment in every worldly truth. My intention was to show
that Being and the subject are always richer and deeper
in their appearing than that which can appear and that
the historicity of the truth and its element of perspective, which are conditioned in this way, and its dialogical essence are ultimately a dialogue that has been going
on from the very outset between Creator and creature

Rudolf Kassner is perhaps the man who has carried out the best preliminary studies here.

[10] *Wahrheit. Erstes Buch: Wahrheit der Welt* (Einsiedeln: Benziger, 1947;
2d ed., Einsiedeln: Johannes Verlag, 1985) (= *Theologik*, vol. 1: *Wahrheit
der Welt*).

and that the human act of seeking is enclosed a priori in the state of being safe in God and of having been found by God. Naturally, this means that an indirect light from Christian revelation falls on every object of philosophy; but in any case, philosophy outside the Christian sphere was something alive only where it was at the same time theology; in the Christian sphere, it can remain alive only in a passionate dialogue with the theology of revelation, indeed, in the willingness to allow its own hidden theological implications to be demonstrated by the latter.

The idea that Christ is the converging point of all the paths of God presses on, however, toward a still more radical unfolding, since the *eis Christon* of the entire creation demands a corresponding protology, a doctrine of predestination and of the primal state and an eschatology in which the judgment and redemption of creation by Christ (who has become the measure of the cosmos through his divinity and through his humanity, through his life and through his death, through his descent to hell and through his Ascension to heaven) is made known as the event that once and for all crosses beyond the relationship between God and man that existed in the Old Covenant and yet at the same time is new for every person at every moment. Almost my entire work (at best with the exception of the Augustine books) can be read and understood under this heading: as an attempt not to underestimate the utterly mysterious step that revelation takes beyond the eschatology of the Old Covenant (which must be understood prophetically!) into the eschatology of the New and eternal Covenant.

3. All of this demanded a wide-ranging theology of the Word, elements of which had already been provided by my patristic studies, on the one side, and the book *The*

Theology of Karl Barth, on the other. In *Origenes, Geist und Feuer. Ein Aufbau aus seinen Schriften* (*Origen: Spirit and Fire: A Thematic Anthology of His Writings*),[11] we find the most logically consistent theology of the patristic age, with over one thousand texts, purified from gnostic additions, an almost inexhaustible source of spiritual and theological stimulus for all later Christian thinking. The summarizing study "Le Mystérion d'Origène"[12] shows to what an extent the Incarnation of the Word, and thereby the penetration of the flesh by Spirit, has an all-embracing Catholic-sacramental character here: theology appears in this book as the doctrine of the appearing and communication of God through his eternal Word, which becomes sound and writing in the Old Covenant, in order then to become fully flesh and sacrament in the New and to bring about the turning of the world to the Father in Resurrection, Ascension and the outpouring of the Spirit. This vision is brought to perfection in the two speculative pupils of Origen: first in Gregory of Nyssa, *Présence et pensée. Essai sur la philosophie religieuse de Grégoire de Nysse* (Presence and thought. Essay on the religious philosophy of Gregory of Nyssa);[13] *Der versiegelte Quell. Auslegung des Hohen Liedes* (The sealed fountain: Commentary on the Song of Songs),[14] where a philosophy of "becoming" is developed with such a dynamism and openness that it

[11] *Origenes, Geist und Feuer. Ein Aufbau aus seinen Werken* (Salzburg: Otto Müller, 1938; revised and expanded ed., 1953). English translation: *Origen: Spirit and Fire: A Thematic Anthology of His Writings* (Washington, D.C.: Catholic University of America Press, 1984). Cf. also: *Parole et Mystère chez Origène* (Paris: Éditions du Cerf. 1957).

[12] In: *Recherches de science religieuse* 26 and 27; edited as a book by P. Pie Duployé: *Parole et mystère chez Origène* (Paris: Éditions du Cerf, 1957).

[13] Paris: Beauchesne, 1942; 2d ed., 1988.

[14] Gregory of Nyssa, *Der versiegelte Quell. Auslegung des Hohen Liedes*,

has the effect of a Christian anticipation and supersed-
ing of German Idealism and of many of Heidegger's intu-
itions; then in Maximus the Confessor, *Kosmische Liturgie*
(Cosmic liturgy) and *Die gnostischen Centurien des Maximus
Confessor* (The gnostic centuries of Maximus the Confessor),[15] where now, too, the tributaries of Dionysius' theology of the mysteries and the monastic theology of Evagrius Ponticus unite in the theologian of Chalcedon to
form a universal cosmic Christology. This brings a form
of thought to maturity; its further path, up to Baader and
Soloviev, has often been described already. The study of
Hamann and Friedrich Schlegel were to prove a fruitful
addition to this, as well as the study of the Jewish (Martin
Buber) and Protestant theology of the Word (*Karl Barth.
Darstellung und Deutung seiner Theologie* [*The Theology of
Karl Barth*]).[16] The dialogue with Buber in the Catholic
sphere is already long overdue; my wish is to conduct
it with all caution and reverence from the standpoint of
the Holy People chosen by the Word to hear and obey
—a standpoint that is unspeakably important for us, too,

---

abbreviated translation with introduction (Salzburg: Otto Müller, 1939)
3d ed., Sigillum Collection 3 (Einsiedeln: Johannes Verlag, 1954). New
ed., revised according to the critical edition, Christliche Meister Collection 23.

[15] *Kosmische Liturgie, Höhe und Krise des griechischen Weltbildes bei Maximus Confessor* (Freiburg: Herder, 1941); 2d, completely revised ed.,
with two further studies: *Die gnostischen Centurien des Maximus Confessor* and *Das Scholienwerk des Johannes von Scythopolis* (Einsiedeln: Johannes Verlag, 1961; 3d ed., 1988).

[16] See n. 7 above. See also some clarifications of expressions that were
misunderstood: "Der Begriff der Natur in der Theologie. Eine Diskus-
sion zwischen Hans Urs von Balthasar und Engelbert Gutwenger, S.J.",
in: *Zweitschrift für katholische Theologie* 75:452–61.

although it has been underestimated in an incomprehensible manner, a standpoint that is ever prophetic and eschatological in the sense of Romans 11. This people is the bearer of the promises, the Servant of Yahweh, the holy stem on which the Church of the Gentile peoples has been grafted. Here, again and again, lies the true, fruitful, both theological and historical point of access to the theology of the Word. —In a theology of the Word, it would be necessary to broaden the dialogue with Barth, which hitherto has been conducted above all in the themes of fundamental theology (*analogia entis et fidei*, knowledge and faith, the question of the philosophical presupposition in theological thinking, the dialectic of the concept of nature), to take in the question of the ecclesial character and sacramentality of the Word of God. But neither the Fathers nor Buber nor Barth, neither Hamann nor (unfortunately) Catholic Romanticism communicate to us the outlines of the Catholic theology of the Word that is awaited today, a theology on which generations of theologians would have to work. *Inter alia*, it would be necessary to develop a theology (which even today's exegesis could acknowledge) of the literal and spiritual senses of Scripture, according to the scheme from 2 Corinthians 3–5 (Old Covenant—New Covenant—eternity: cf. "Die Schrift als Gottes Wort" ("The Word, Scripture and Tradition")[17] and the translation of Henri de Lubac

---

[17] In: *Schweizer Rundschau* 49:428–42. Included under the title "Wort, Schrift, Tradition" in: *Verbum Caro*. Skizzen zur Theologie I (Einsiedeln: Johannes Verlag, 1960; 2d ed., 1965). English translation: in two volumes: *Word and Revelation*, Essays in Theology 1 (New York: Herder and Herder, 1964) and *Word and Redemption*, Essays in Theology 2 (New York: Herder and Herder, 1965); new edition, in one volume: *The Word Made Flesh*. Explorations in Theology 1 (San Francisco:

Le Sens spirituel de l'Écriture (The spiritual sense of Scripture),[18] and this doctrine in turn would have to have a christological structure. Here it would be necessary to give an interpretation also of the entire existence of Jesus Christ, and not only his explicit teachings as the Word of God: and specifically, at its summit, in the flesh.

In many lectures about the dramatic character of that which is Christian, I have attempted to gain access to the mysteries of revelation through the parable of the (Christian) theater. The "world theater" is understood here as the serious play that is put on the stage in the parable of an "economic Trinity" by author, actor and director (I hear Kassner's warning perfectly well!), and human, Christian existence is understood as a "role", just as Calderon, the greatest Christian dramatist, understood it. His *Autos sacramentales* are the organic transformation of the abstract-essential thought forms of Thomas Aquinas into the character of "event" proper to the stage, as well as the transmutation of all secular and classical materials, which are made transparent to the events of salvation: a play in view of the eternal Eucharist, which rests in the mystery. This parable would be very fruitful and would offer the advantage—just as with the Catholic music of Haydn and Mozart—of being conducted from the very outset in an unpolemic, natively Catholic sphere without any "existentialist" attack on the essential thought forms.

Ignatius Press, 1989). The English title of this essay is "The Word, Scripture, and Tradition" (pp. 11–26).

[18] *Der geistliche Sinn der Schrift*, with introduction (Einsiedeln: Johannes Verlag, 1952); an excerpt from Henri de Lubac, *Geist aus der Geschichte. Das Schriftverständnis des Origenes* (Einsiedeln: Johannes Verlag, 1968).

The primacy of the Word of God in prayer, the primacy of role and representation in life of the Word that has gone forth: both of these frame the concept of mission. Vis-à-vis the believing subject, this is objective Spirit, but not in the sense of the philosophers; rather, as the gift (*charisma*) of the Holy Spirit, who is first of all the Spirit of the Church of Christ, that Spirit who unfolds the fullness of Christ in his gifts of life, which he pours into the members of the Body that is Christ's Bride.

1. Thus the first task is to recover for the Church Hegel's objective Spirit, which has declined into the state; or, in other words, to recover the totality of the Church's holiness, as this can be seen from the missions of holiness in Church history (as the New Testament counterpart to the great missions in the Old Testament).[19] At the service of this idea, the collection Menschen der Kirche in Zeugnis und Urkunde (Men of the Church)[20] was begun, with the intention above all of presenting anew in their own words those saints who have made their mark externally, too: Augustine, the Church Father who struggles for the pure form of the Church,[21] Joan of Arc and Catherine of Siena, Thomas More and Vincent de Paul, the great founders of Orders, Ignatius, Newman.

[19] Once again, works by Adrienne von Speyr stand in the background here: an interpretation of John 21:11, in terms of the primary ecclesial missions, a wealth of descriptions of the essence of individual commissions of holiness in the Church, a richly developed teaching about ecclesial contemplation, action and passion.

[20] Volumes 1–10 (Einsiedeln: Benziger, 1942–1951). In part in: Neuer Folge (NF).

[21] Cf. *Abendländische Kirchenfreiheit. Dokumente über Kirche und Staat*, trans. with introduction by Hugo Rahner (Einsiedeln: Benziger, 1943).

The new collection *Sigillum*,[22] in the same spirit but in shorter presentations, will give a rich and vivid expression of the fullness of the Church's holiness; the treasures of the Church, from the Church Fathers up to the present day, including mediaeval and Baroque mysticism and the traditional theology accessible to wider groups of people, are to be made accessible to today's Christian. Once again it is Church Fathers, above all, Origen, Maximus and Augustine, who serve to establish the chief aim: that *Theologie und Heiligkeit*[23] ("theology and holiness") ought to contribute a deeper fruitfulness to one another. Is not theology, too, a charism, and is not a life in Christ a new pointer to the Word? At the service of the same idea stands the meditation, which is especially urgent today, on the states in the Church,[24] in which the objective life forms of existence in the Church—as we know, the word "state" carries its own historical burden—are investigated in terms of their original existence in the Gospel and in their historical development, so that they may appear in their first purity to today's Christian, who is looking for paths to imitate.

2. In each individual case, one must demonstrate the superiority of mission over "psychology", so that the whole project becomes a concentric onslaught against

[22] Einsiedeln: Johannes Verlag, from 1954.

[23] This connection is illuminated by an article ("Theologie und Heiligkeit") in: *Wort und Wahrheit* 3:881ff., French text in: *Dieu vivant* 12:17–21. Included and given greater depth in: "Was soll Theologie? Ihr Ort und ihre Gestalt im Leben der Kirche", in: *Wort und Wahrheit* 8:325ff; French text in appendix to *Théologie de l'histoire* (Plon, 1955; 3d ed., Paris: Fayard, 1970).

[24] *Christlicher Stand* (Einsiedeln: Johannes Verlag, 1977; 2d ed., 1981). English translation: *The Christian State of Life* (San Francisco: Ignatius Press, 1983).

modern subjectivism and "personalism" in the religious sphere. I study the list of famous subjective writers (Augustine—Pascal—Kierkegaard—Dostoyevsky)—cf. "Psychologie der Heiligen?" (Psychology of the saints?)[25] —when it is a question of recovering the subjective dimension in the ecclesial-objective dimension. This is the aim of the three selections from Augustine; it is seen most clearly in the *Confessions*,[26] where it is shown that this greatest monument of religious subjectivity can be understood and accepted only as the retrieval into the Church (*confessio* as confession of sin) of the lost subjectivity of Augustine's youth and as the opening (*confessio* as praise, as *opus Dei*) to the great future theology of the *De Trinitate, Enarrationes in Psalmos*, the commentaries on Genesis, Paul and John, and *Civitas Dei*. The abbreviated translation of the commentary on the Psalms[27] aims to realize precisely this becoming one with the Church, for King David's confessions here become a dialogue between Christ and the Church. A fortiori, the selection from the *Sermones* (Augustine, *Das Antlitz der Kirche* [The face of the Church][28] allows the surging symphony of Augustine's soul to flow into the service of God within the Catholic Church.

In the case of Origen, Maximus and Irenaeus (*Irenäus, Geduld des Reifens* [*The Scandal of the Incarnation*]),[29] it was

[25] In: *Schweizer Rundschau* 48:644–52.

[26] Fischer-Bücherei, 1955. My own translation with a new introduction: *Die Bekenntnisse*, Christliche Meister Collection 25 (Einsiedeln: Johannes Verlag, 1985; 2d ed., 1988.)

[27] Augustine, *Über die Psalmen* (Leipzig: Hegner, 1936); 2d ed., Christliche Meister Collection 20 (Einsiedeln: Johannes Verlag, 1983).

[28] *Das Antlitz der Kirche* (Einsiedeln: Benziger, 1942; 2d ed., 1955).

[29] *Irenäus, Geduld des Reifens. Die christliche Antwort auf den gnostischen*

not necessary to begin by making this reduction; but it seemed imperative in the case of *Therese von Lisieux. Geschichte einer Sendung* (*Thérèse of Lisieux* in *Two Sisters in the Spirit*)[30] ("Story of a mission": the title was set in antithesis to the "Story of a *soul*"). It was necessary to set up the counterweight of the "little way" and of the simple fulfillment of a commission against the ever-threatening danger in Carmel and in the Church of a one-sided exaltation of the grandiose subjectivity of the Great Teresa and of the spiritual radicalism of John of the Cross so that these become the absolute canon of mysticism and of holiness. This counterweight lay in the mission of the supernatural state of childhood (in antithesis to the intoxication of worldly and churchly "maturity" today) and of the mysterious preponderance of the Father's mercy in all judgment (James 2:13). From Thérèse, the path led on farther, first to the hieratic-biblical stance of *Elisabeth von Dijon und ihre geistliche Sendung* (*Elizabeth of the Trinity* in *Two Sisters in the Spirit*),[31] where the motif of life

---

Mythos des 2. Jahrhunderts, Klosterberg Collection (Basel: Schwabe, 1943). 2d improved ed.: Sigillum Collection 6 (Einsiedeln: Johannes Verlag, 1956). New ed.: *Gott in Fleisch und Blut. Ein Durchblick in Texten*, Christliche Meister Collection 11, with revised introduction (Einsiedeln: Johannes Verlag, 1982). English translation: *The Scandal of the Incarnation: Irenaeus against the Heresies*, selected and with an introduction by Hans Urs von Balthasar (San Francisco: Ignatius Press, 1990).

[30] Cologne and Olten: Hegner-Bücherei, 1950; Einsiedeln: Johannes Verlag, 1970. English translation: *Thérèse of Lisieux. The Story of a Mission* (New York: Sheed and Ward, 1954). Together with *Elisabeth von Dijon und ihre geistliche Sendung* in: *Schwestern im Geist. Therese von Lisieux und Elisabeth von Dijon*, 4th ed. (1990). English translation: *Two Sisters in the Spirit* (San Francisco: Ignatius Press, 1992).

[31] Cologne and Olten: Hegner-Bücherei, 1952. English translation:

on the basis of blessed predestination made possible an
encounter from Carmel with the fundamental motif of
Karl Barth and where in the *Laus Gloriae* the antithesis
between Carmel and the objectivist-liturgical mysticism
of Bingen and Helfta was resolved into a harmony (cf.
Mechthild of Hackeborn, *Das Buch vom strömenden Lob*
[*The Book of Special Grace*]).[32] The path next led to Charles
Péguy's poetic unfolding of the commission of Lisieux:
Le Mystère des saints innocents,[33] *Le Porche du mystère de le
deuxième vertu*[34] and *Wir stehen alle an der Front*;[35] and an
interpretation of Péguy's eschatology in the three ver-
sions of his *Jeanne d'Arc* most decidedly belongs here
too.

In parallel to this, and in an innermost connection with
Little Thérèse and Péguy, I had also to lead back an apparently wildly subjective man to his ecclesial-objective
presuppositions: Bernanos[36] (cf. G. Bernanos: *Das sanfte
Erbarmen*, Letters of the poet,[37] and his *Die Geduld der*

Elizabeth of Dijon: An Interpretation of Her Spiritual Mission (New York:
Pantheon, 1956). See n. 30, above.

[32] With preface, Sigillum Collection 4 (Einsiedeln: Johannes Verlag,
1955); 2d ed., Christliche Meister Collection 31 (1987).

[33] Charles Péguy, *Mysterium der unschuldigen Kinder*, unpublished translation.

[34] Charles Péguy, *Das Tor zum Geheimnis der Hoffnung* (Lucerne:
Stocker, 1943; 2d revised ed., Einsiedeln: Johannes Verlag, 1980).

[35] Charles Péguy, *Wir stehen alle an der Front*. Selection from his prose,
with introduction. Christ heute 3/3 (Einsiedeln: Johannes Verlag,
1952).

[36] Under the title *Gelebte Kirche: Bernanos* (Cologne and Olten: Hegner-Bücherei, 1954; 3d ed., 1988). French translation by M. de Gandil-
lac (Paris: Éditions du Seuil, 1955; 2d ed., n.d.).

[37] Georges Bernanos, *Das sanfte Erbarmen: Briefe des Dichters*, with preface (Einsiedeln: Johannes Verlag, 1951).

Armen. Neue Briefe,[38] and his *Predigt eines Atheisten am Fest der Kleinen Therese*).[39] For this sufferer is and understands himself only as a man of the Church; the subjective dimension of his heroes can only be grasped as the unfolding—affirmed in the freedom of the spirit, or else denied and checked—of the sacramental ecclesial reality, above all, that of confession, the Eucharist, priestly ordination and anointing; his novels are expositions of a lived theology of the sacraments. He was given the gift of proclaiming in the thundering sound of bells what the Carmelites adore in silence. And even if he lives in anxiety, and anxiety becomes a medium of knowledge for him, it is only incidentally that he gives the answer to Heidegger: his concern is not philosophizing but the salvation of the world through the Church, and the dignity of the Church through the salvation of every man who knows about the honor and dignity of the Christian. I had already attempted in the little book *Der Christ und die Angst* (The Christian and anxiety)[40] to bring back the most important phenomenon of modern "psychology" into the biblical perspective of Old and New Testaments and into the perspective of the Church.

3. All this would require a final interpretation in a history of Christian mysticism and of spirituality as a whole, under the leitmotiv of mission. Thus: mysticism as charism; taking up afresh that early Christian theme that broke off for the first time with the fiasco of Montanism

[38] Georges Bernanos, *Die Geduld der Armen. Neue Briefe*, with preface (Einsiedeln: Johannes Verlag, 1954).

[39] Georges Bernanos, *Predigt eines Atheisten am Fest der Kleinen Therese* (Einsiedeln: Johannes Verlag, 1954).

[40] *Der Christ und die Angst* (Einsiedeln: Johannes Verlag, 1951; 6th ed., 1989).

and suffered a second dramatic shipwreck with Joachim of Fiore and the Franciscan Spirituals. Both times, the fundamental error was the subjectivization of the ecclesial spirit, which was detached from the regulation of the Church's official ministry and the traditional preaching of the Faith. Where could one find a safer point to start than in Thomas Aquinas' treatise on the charisms? Now it can be read in a detailed commentary[41] in such a way that the three places where Thomas discusses mysticism —the charismatic dimension with the central concept of the prophecy of the Old and New Testaments, the gifts of the Holy Spirit as the supernatural perfection of the virtues in the sphere of experience, and contemplation —open out onto one another and are set in mutual relationship. In the background stood Augustine's wholly forgotten treatise on prophecy and vision, *De Genesi ad litteram liber 12*[42] and a rich early scholastic tradition that is almost completely unpublished. The plan of evaluating this tradition and of expanding it to a newly conceived intellectual history of Christian spirituality can be envisaged only by a team of like-minded persons. Indications and building-blocks for this will be made available in *Sigillum*.[43]

---

[41] Volume 23 of the German-Latin edition of Thomas: *Besondere Gnadengaben und die zwei Wege menschlichen Lebens* (F. H. Kerle-A. Pustet, 1954).

[42] *Aurelius Augustinus, Psychologie und Mystik*, translation and introduction together with M. E. Korger. Sigillum Collection 18 (Einsiedeln: Johannes Verlag, 1960).

[43] Introduction to Gregory of Nyssa, *Der versiegelte Quell* (1954); to Mechthild of Hackeborn (1955); postscript to the *Exerzitien* (1954); preface to the new arrangement of the text of Louis Lallemant, S.J., ed. by Robert Rast (Lucerne, 1948); postscript to the selection from the *Cherubinischer Wandersmann*, in: *Dich auftun wie die Rose*, Sigillum Col-

None of this is meant to lead to a devaluation of Christian interiority: all that is ever intended is to break open hollow human subjectivity to the clear fullness of the Church, which is the one Bride, in whose mystery everyone who loves must participate. I discovered this Catholicism of fullness in the flowing riches of Henri de Lubac's *Catholicisme*, and I saw at once the urgent necessity of translating it into German.[44] Here the whole revealed itself as living, sovereign and straightforward; here, knowledge of the tradition was no dry, historical hair-splitting but something as natural as the movement of one's own limbs.

3

The Church draws to herself all the truth, beauty and freedom of creation; in Augustine's vision, which has remained determinative until the present day (Newman!), the history of the world is a dialogue between creation and covenant, kingdom of the world and Kingdom of God, Church and culture.

1. The Church in the New Covenant fulfills the essence of the synagogue, namely, to be the people of the promise, the people for all. As the anticipation of the universal Kingdom of God, the Church always transcends her visible form—which, as such, is founded by Christ and is not

---

lection 3 (1954); cf. new ed.: *Cherubinischer Wandersmann*, Christliche Meister Collection 6, and so on. In addition, there are the cycles of lectures on the intellectual history of mysticism.

[44] Henri de Lubac, *Katholizismus als Gemeinschaft* (Einsiedeln: Benziger, 1943); 2d ed. (Einsiedeln: Johannes Verlag, 1970) under the title: *Glauben aus der Liebe*.

to be dissolved—into an (eschatological) totality. This
is how the Greek Fathers saw her, as the sacrament of
the redeemed cosmos, as the light of Christ progressively
shedding its rays into all the darknesses of the world. This
is why the Church has an open cosmic form in Maximus,
just as the cosmos has a hidden ecclesial form. This understanding of the Church is the fundamental religious
and poetical experience in two modern Catholic poets:
Paul Claudel, who certainly cannot be accused of a lack
of sensitivity to the visible, sacramental and hierarchical
Church, can breathe only in the air of the world-totality.
This makes the extraordinary conception of his *Soulier
de satin* (*Satin Slipper*),[45] despite all the objections that
can be made to it otherwise, an event in the history of
Catholic poetry. At one stroke, he has swept away all
the sacristy atmosphere of the nineteenth-century French
Church, which withdrew, genteel and offended, from the
secularized modern world. This great roar of ocean and
organ must also flow over the careworn, furrowed brows
of the German Catholic Kierkegaardians and their sour
problems with words, language and style, otherwise they
would not be worthy to invoke the name of Newman.
What right has this Protestant tearing apart of the aesthetic
and ethical-religious dimensions, appealing to a sense of
tragedy, to exist in our domain, which is the domain of
Augustine, of Dante, of Fra Angelico, of Mozart? For is
the fact that great art is Christian a *problem*? The same
waves swell through the *Cinq grandes odes*,[46] the mighti-

[45] Paul Claudel, *Der seidene Schuh* (Salzburg: Otto Müller, 1939; 11th
ed., 1987).
[46] Paul Claudel, *Fünf grosse Oden* (Freiburg: Herder, 1939; 3d ed.,
Einsiedeln: Johannes Verlag, 1964). Cf. also *Gesammelte Werke*, vol. 1:
Lyrik (Einsiedeln: Benziger; Heidelberg: F. H. Kerle, 1963).

est of which seems to me to be *Les Muses*; we find it again in the Poésies diverse (*Vermischte Gedichte*),[47] where the solemn Ode to Dante and the captivating poem about the Great Teresa form the main center of emphasis. Everywhere, even in *Le Chemin de la Croix*,[48] there is the same mixture of eros (as the bitter solitude of the wanderer) and agape (as the sweet, relaxed gesture that understands and embraces). The boundary became clear to me when I translated *L'Annonce faite è Marie*:[49] the symbolism of the turn of the century threatens to obscure the genuine dialectic of the ecclesial states of life and, even more deeply, the dialectic of the two Testaments; and its most gripping effects are attained by means that are not wholly pure.

While Claudel nourishes his poetic work on Thomas Aquinas and again and again on the Bible, the Christian Reinhold Schneider makes the act of transcendence into the sphere of history. Here, as nowhere else, Christianity once again light and the judgment of every event within and outside the Church; the solitary, adoring act of listening to the Word of God was the primal cell of all fruitful action; the renunciation carried out by those chosen and sent was the inner form of all world governance and conquest. Nowhere else did I find in such a pure form what I sought everywhere, namely, the anti-psychological instinct, the native knowledge of roles, service and mission,

[47] Paul Claudel, *Gedichte*, Klosterberg Collection (Basel: Schwabe, 1942). 3d ed.: in the series Christ heute 3/1 (Einsiedeln: Johannes Verlag, 1953), under the title *Der Wanderer in der Flamme*. Cf. *Gesammelte Werke*, vol. 1: *Lyrik*.

[48] Paul Claudel, *Der Kreuzweg* (Lucerne, Stocker, 1943). From 1957, in: *Corona Benignitatis Anni Dei*, 3d ed. (Einsiedeln: Johannes Verlag, 1965). Cf. also *Gesammelte Werke*, vol. 1: *Lyrik*.

[49] Paul Claudel, *Mariä Verkündigung* (Lucerne: Stocker, 1943).

a Catholic form that does not live in monastic fortresses and "political Catholicisms", perhaps not even in organized Orders at all, but in the souls of those who have received commissions, whether these be kings or founders or simple laymen. Thus the book *Reinhold Schneider. Sein Weg und sein Work* (Reinhold Schneider: His life and his work) became a gesture of gratitude to a friend.[50]

Ultimately, one will find the same fundamental act of crossing the boundaries in Bernanos too; he, too, is one who works on the basis of prayer, a politician out of ethical conviction, a poet out of a religious responsibility, with the same tragic pathos of the knowledge of what is transitory, with the same courage (which has grown rather rare in the Catholic Church today) not only to think the truth but to say it simply and without bitterness.

The forty-four small volumes of the collection *Christ heute* (The Christian today) that have so far appeared stand in the service of dialogue with our own time and of the inner clarification and strengthening that are a necessary preparation for this. They wish to awaken the same general impression: that the Church is young, without being a product of contemporary relevance—as young as ever she was.

2. The Church, which is sent into the world, owes it to this world to find an intellectual language that can in principle be understood by the present period. She must stand in dialogue with the thought of the age—of every age. The Church Fathers and the theologians of the high scholastic period remain the model for this; Erich Przy-

---

[50] *Reinhold Schneider. Sein Leben und sein Werk* (Cologne and Olten: Hegner-Bücherei, 1953). 2d revised and expanded ed.: *Nochmals— Reinhold Schneider* (Einsiedeln: Johannes Verlag, 1991).

wara and Joseph Maréchal, with their skill at understanding interpretation and transposition, have been masters
for our own age.[51] In the three volumes of *Apokalypse
der deutschen Seele. Studien zu einer Lehre von letzten Haltungen* (Apocalypse of the German soul: Toward a theory
of fundamental orientations),[52] I began, in keeping with
the training in German studies I received, with German
Idealism (which has produced our best: Schlegel, Baader,
Görres, Möhler, Staudenmaier and the tragic Günther).
The aim here was not a theoretical discussion but evidence of the point at which in each case—voluntarily
or under compulsion—the opening to the ultimate dimension, namely, Christ, takes place. I still stand today
by much of the contents of this forgotten book; and it
will not be difficult to perceive the places where I was
most deeply affected: by the late Fichte, by Novalis and
Hölderlin and again and again by Goethe. The Schiller
of the *Maltheser* kept me from closing the dossier on the
aesthetic Idealists; in Goethe, I love the late Aristotelian
whose unswerving objectivity could even embrace a *Tasso*
and a *Faust* and cope with them, who uses all the trem-
bling of the soul, all the resonance of the inner depths,
to form the song of praise of righteous and good exis-

[51] Cf. my: "Von den Aufgaben der katholischen Philosophie in der
Zeit", in: *Annalen der philosophischen Gesellschaft der Innerschweiz* (De-
cember/January 1946/1947), 1–38.

[52] *Apokalypse der deutschen Seele. Studien zu einer Lehre von letzten Haltungen*, vol. 1: *Der deutsche Idealismus*; vol. 2: *Im Zeichen Nietzsches*; vol.
3: *Die Vergöttlichung des Todes* (Salzburg: A. Pustet, 1937–1939). New
ed. of vol. 1: *Prometheus. Studien zur Geschichte des deutschen Idealismus*
(Heidelberg: F. H. Kerle, 1947). This alteration of the title of the first
volume was made on the basis of the assertion then made in America
that, for the time being, a "German soul" was not to be allowed to
exist.

tences—and nothing will be able to separate me from
Mozart and from the highest creations of Haydn, from
the ever-new and terrible experience that there are things
too beautiful for our world. And yet one should not fail
at any point, and the work was supposed to be devoted
to evidence of the Promethean inspiration from Lessing
to Rilke. (What difficult work the angels will have to
do on the Last Day, when they must gather up God's
truth so far outside and must surgically remove it from
hearts where it has never lived except in coexistence
with darkness!) Nietzsche, in his ceaseless, hidden dialogue with Kierkegaard and Dostoyevsky, revealed to me
the meaning of the dialogic relationship between world
views, especially between Christian and non-Christian
world views. In the second part, an avenue of approach
to the Spirit and its depths had to be prepared once again
from the philosophy of life; I saw this achieved anew in
the demonic brilliance of Scheler and in the confrontation between Heidegger and Rilke in a way that has not
been surpassed up to the present day. After this, it remained only to speak with Karl Barth; the brief presentation later became the book, likewise going back explicitly to the point of departure in Idealism. The dialogue
was continued in a looser form by the fifty volumes of
the *Sammlung Klosterberg, Europäische Reihe* (Klosterberg
collection. European series),[53] of which I must mention
above all Edgar Salin's volume on Plato, Emil Staiger's
Sophocles and the contributions by Carl J. Burckhardt,
Huizinga, Claudel and Buber, as well as the structured selections from Goethe, Novalis, Nietzsche and Borchardt.
The theme of the little book *Schleifung der Bastionen (Raz-*

[53] Basel, Schwabe.

ing the Bastions)[54] was likewise the Church in dialogue with the world; the title has perhaps too provocative a ring, since the book contains only the assertion that the Church should not erect barriers to protect herself from the world. A book about the position of man in the cosmos today, which will shortly be published,[55] will attempt to set out why this is more true of our age in the world's history than ever.

3. All this would remain mere literary chatter were it not at the service of, and obedient to, an ecclesial action that has been assigned to me, which I myself have not chosen. This is the center; everything else, even if developed earlier, has been placed around it. The mystery that starts from John and Ignatius and is to be lived as service and mission within the Church, but (more explicitly than in earlier times) in the world too, becomes here the as yet unnameable ideal of the Christian: to follow the counsels of Jesus in the midst of the world, without abandoning one's post. This is not the religious state in the old sense; it is the radicalism of the gospel in the particularity of our time. *Der Laie und der Ordensstand* (The laity and the religious state)[56] indicated the first, as yet imprecise, outlines of this; the very title is open to misunderstanding, and the whole work needs to be redone, needs to be thought out still more simply and directly. It is only lived experience that can suf-

[54] Einsiedeln: Johannes Verlag; 5th ed., 1989. English translation: *Razing the Bastions* (San Francisco: Ignatius Press, 1993).

[55] *Die Gottesfrage des heutigen Menschen* (Vienna: Herold, 1956). English translation: *Science, Religion and Christianity* (Westminster, Md.: Newman Press, 1958); and *The God Question and Modern Man* (New York: Seabury Press, 1967).

[56] Einsiedeln: Johannes Verlag, 1942; 2d ed., Freiburg: Herder, 1949.

fice now, not any written program. It is indeed true that
the Church, as *Provida Mater*, has already had the fore-
sight to create sufficient canonical frameworks for this
form of life, but we still lack calm experience and a comprehensive spirituality. This will need to be very open
and all-embracing, going as far as a *coincidentia opposito-
rum* that can be realized only from within and in the
course of life: from the outside, it can be only the object of doubt and criticism. And one should always note
that a qualitative mission in the Church, apostolate in the
strong sense of this term (and, indeed, basically already
the study of theology and the *missio canonica*), demands
an asceticism of the Christian, a renunciation as Christ
understands this: otherwise the salt loses its taste, and
Christianity becomes one harmless action among others.
Nothing today should frighten us as much as the Christian ignorance of so many laymen who imagine they are
"mature", whereby indispensable elements of the innermost kernel of the gospel threaten to be cast onto the
scrap-heap. But this renunciation can take on an intensi-
fied form today, if one who is called and abandons everything must stay at his post in the world for the sake of
the Kingdom of God. The deeper action is to penetrate,
the deeper must be the preceding and accompanying contemplation. The more free, virile and responsible Christian action and decision in the world is to become, the
more must it be opened inward in listening obedience.
The unity of obedience and free responsibility, simply
lived out, would be one of the most fruitful foundations
of a fresh flowering of theological thinking in the Church
and about her—if it is at all the plan of Providence to
give the Church of the near future much theology, and not

rather the "demonstration of spirit and power" anew[57] in the Holy Spirit—in the midst of the world, not of the world.

[57] 1 Cor 2:4.

III

In Retrospect

1965

1. The Salient Point

Ten years ago an account of my literary work could be constructed on an objective and dogmatic foundation. In an earlier survey of my work, *A Short Guide to My Books*,[1] it was possible to begin theologically with Christ and the Church before addressing the position of the Church in the world and the practical tasks that lay before her. The subsequent changes in Church and Christendom require us to reverse this order and to set out now from what in the earlier piece was placed at the end as challenge and goal: the driving entelechy of the task that is given us. The latter had been at work long before the author ever took up pen, and, at the time of his first publications [*Veröffentlichungen*], it remained undisclosed [*unveröffentlicht*] even to him. His entire literary output will ultimately have been but a means to a strange *Meaning*, who, with his coming, is free to discard as past everything that was merely "way".

The last ten years—inspiring both joy and alarm—

Rechenschaft translated by Kenneth Batinovich, N.S.M. and Fr. Brian McNeil, C.R.V. This article originally appeared in English in *Communio* 2 (1975): 197–220. It was reprinted in *The Analogy of Beauty: The Theology of Hans Urs von Balthasar*, edited by John Riches (Edinburgh: T. & T. Clark, 1986), and revised to conform to the German edition of *Mein Werk—Durchblicke* (Freiburg and Einsiedeln: Johannes Verlag, 1990).

[1] "Kleiner Lage plan zu meinen Büchern", see Chapter 2, above.

have seen the real decision ineluctably emerge from its
preliminary forms. We were a fine group, resolute and
exposed, and it was clear to us from the beginning that
the bastions of anxiety that the Church had contrived
to protect herself from the world would have to be de-
molished; the Church had to be freed to become herself and open to the whole and undivided world for its
mission. For the meaning of Christ's coming is to save
the *world* and to open for the whole of it the way to
the Father; the Church is only a means, a radiance that
through preaching, example and discipleship spreads out
from the God-man into every sphere. This passion ral-
lied us young theologians (Fessard, Bouillard, Daniélou
and many others) in Lyons around our older friend and
master Henri de Lubac, from whom we gained an understanding of the Greek Fathers, the philosophical mysticism of Asia and the phenomenon of modern atheism;
to him my patristic studies owe their initial spark. For
patristics meant to us a Christendom that still carried its
thoughts into the limitless space of the nations and still
trusted in the world's salvation. At that time, I conceived
the plan of a closely woven trilogy on the writings of
Origen, Gregory of Nyssa and Maximus the Confessor,
of which unfortunately only fragments were completed.[2]
This passion made the radiant openness of de Lubac's

---

[2] *Origenes, Geist und Feuer. Ein Aufbau aus seinen Werken* (Salzburg:
Otto Müller, 1938; revised and expanded ed., 1953). English translation: *Origen: Spirit and Fire: A Thematic Anthology of His Writings* (Washington, D.C.: Catholic University of America Press, 1984). Cf. also:
Parole et mystère chez Origène (Paris: Éditions du Cerf, 1957). Gregory
of Nyssa, *Der versiegelte Quell. Auslegung des Hohen Liedes*, abbreviated
translation with introduction (Salzburg: Otto Müller, 1939); 3d ed.,

Catholicisme a fundamental book for us, and I translated it shortly afterward;[3] it led us to read Claudel's *Soulier de satin* (*The Satin Slipper*) together on free days on the hills overlooking the Saône—the translation of this was almost my first literary attempt.[4]

The work by Maximus did not receive the title *Kosmische Liturgie* (Cosmic liturgy) without serious premeditation,[5] and out of contemplation of the cosmic Christ grew the hymns entitled *Das Herz der Welt* (*Heart of the World*)[6] as well as the book of aphorisms called *Das Weizenkorn* (The grain of wheat).[7] During my semester vacations alongside my work on *Stimmen der Zeit* in Munich, — where I also spent two years on completion of my studies

---

Sigillum Collection 3 (Einsiedeln: Johannes Verlag, 1954). New ed., revised according to the critical edition, Christliche Meister Collection 23. Cf. also: *Présence et pensée. Essai sur la philosophie religieuse de Grégoire de Nysse* (Paris: Beauchesne, 1942; 2d ed., 1988). *Kosmische Liturgie. Höhe und Krise des griechischen Weltbildes bei Maximus Confessor* (Freiburg: Herder, 1941); 2d, completely revised ed., with two further studies: *Die gnostischen Centurien des Maximus Confessor* and *Das Scholienwerk des Johannes von Scythopolis* (Einsiedeln: Johannes Verlag, 1961; 3d ed., 1988).

[3] Henri de Lubac, *Katholizismus als Gemeinschaft* (Einsiedeln: Benziger, 1943); 2d ed. (Einsiedeln: Johannes Verlag, 1970) under the title: *Glauben aus der Liebe*. English translation: *Catholicism: Christ and the Common Destiny of Man* (San Francisco: Ignatius Press, 1988).

[4] Published in 1939; the text has been polished again and again since then. Paul Claudel, *Der seidene Schuh* (Salzburg: Otto Müller, 1939; 11th ed., 1987).

[5] *Kosmische Liturgie*.

[6] *Das Herz der Welt* (Zurich: Arche Verlag, 1945), 4th ed., with new foreword (Ostfildern: Schwabenverlag, 1988). English translation: *Heart of the World* (San Francisco: Ignatius Press, 1979).

[7] *Das Weizenkorn* (Lucerne: Räber, 1944; 3d ed., Einsiedeln: Johannes Verlag, 1989).

—I worked on the three-volume *Apokalypse der deutschen
Seele* (Apocalypse of the German soul),[8] in which the eschatological thinking of German writers was depicted in
the light of Christ. The encounters with Erich Przywara
and later with Karl Barth—whose universalist doctrine
of predestination confirmed what I had long been looking
for—the collaboration with Karl Rahner on the sketch of
a new dogmatics, the renewed theologizing with Hugo
Rahner in the patristic area: all this strengthened my de-
termination to display the Christian message in its unsur-
passable greatness (*id quo majus cogitari nequit*), because it
is God's human word for the world, God's most humble
service eminently fulfilling every human striving, God's
deepest love in the splendor of his dying so that all might
live beyond themselves for him.

When I moved to Basel in 1940, I undertook in the
same spirit the direction of the *Europäische Reihe* (European series) of the *Sammlung Klosterberg*,[9] designed to pro-
vide, at the end of the chaos of nazism, foundation stones
for a spiritual Europe in an utterly open Christian attitude
that sought to bring together much that was ultimately
affirmative from Sophocles and Plato to Goethe, Novalis and Nerval, Claudel and Buber, Huizinga and Carl
J. Burckhardt; among what I still find valuable today of my
own work, I mention only the selection from Goethe's
lamentations (*Nänie*) and the three pseudonymously published selections from Nietzsche (*Vergeblichkeit, Von Gut*

---

[8] *Apokalypse der deutschen Seele. Studien zu einer Lehre von letzten Haltungen*, vol. 1: *Der deutsche Idealismus*; vol. 2: *Im Zeichen Nietzsches*; vol.
3: *Die Vergöttlichung des Todes* (Salzburg: A. Pustet, 1937–1939). New
ed. of vol. 1: *Prometheus. Studien zur Geschichte des deutschen Idealismus*
(Heidelberg: F. H. Kerle, 1947).

[9] Basel, Schwabe.

und Böse, Vom vornehmen Menschen), which attempted to
extract from the *Antichrist* either what Christians ought to
hear or something for which they themselves must bear
responsibility. Also at that time came my programmatic
little book *Schleifung der Bastionen* (*Razing the Bastions*),[10]
the final and already impatient blast of the trumpet calling for a Church no longer barricaded against the world.
The blast did not die away unheard, but now it forced
the trumpeter himself to reflect more deeply.

Indeed, it was not as though we were unaware that
with an opening to the world, an *aggiornamento*, a broad-
ening of the horizons, a translation of the Christian message into an intellectual language understandable by the
modern world, only half is done. The other half—of at
least equal importance—is a reflection on the specifically
Christian element itself, a purification, a deepening, a
centering of its idea, which alone renders us capable of
representing it, radiating it, translating it believably in the
world. We knew this, for almost all of us were formed
by the *Spiritual Exercises*, the great school of christocentric contemplation, of attention to the pure and personal
word contained in the gospel, of lifelong commitment to
the attempt at following, which for Ignatius is above all
a decision regarding the form that a Christian may lend
in his own life to the Lord's attitude of total and loving
renunciation ("evangelical counsels"). For the so-called
"counsels" of Christ are nothing but the form of his re-
deeming love and apply to every believer, whether religious or layman. I translated the *Exercises* into German[11]
and had the opportunity of giving them some hundred

[10] Einsiedeln: Johannes Verlag, 1942; 2d ed., Freiburg: Herder, 1949.
[11] Ignatius of Loyola, *Die Exerzitien* (Lucerne: Stocker, 1946; 10th
ed., Einsiedeln, Freiburg: Johannes Verlag, 1990).

times: here, if anywhere, is Christian joy. Here, if anywhere, is what it means to be a Christian in its "primordial" sense: effective hearing of the Word who calls and
growth in freedom for the expected response. It is here,
too, that we came closest to the sense and inspiration of
the Reformation, from Luther to Karl Barth.

The last ten years have shown inexorably that the
most dynamic program of openness to the world remains one-sided (and hence becomes exceedingly dan-
gerous) if it does not cultivate with growing awareness
its own distinctive counterpoise and balance: whoever
desires greater action needs better contemplation; whoever wants to play a more formative role must pray and
obey more profoundly; whoever wants to achieve ad-
ditional goals must grasp the uselessness and futility, the
uncalculating and incalculable (hence "unprofitable") nature of the eternal love in Christ, as well as of every love
along the path of Christian discipleship. Whoever wants
to command must have learned to follow in a Christ-like
manner; whoever wants to administer the goods of the
world must first have freed himself from all desire for
possession; whoever wants to show the world Christian
love must have practiced the love of Christ (even in mar-
riage) to the point of pure selflessness. We knew all this
and have always said it. Every program of mission to the
world must at all times contain what Guardini called "the
discernment of what is Christian".

And yet it appears today that many no longer really
know this. What has happened to them? A slight, perhaps only tactically meant displacement in the beginning
—yet the effects are incalculable. For the beginnings are
always decisive; the sequence of almost invisible proto-
decisions forms history, as philosophy shows in its do-

main: Plato's Idea, Thomas' *De ente et essentia*, Descartes' *cogito*, Hegel's *Begriff*. . . . The formulation of the question, I said, was clear to us: the world is the goal of the redemption wrought by Christ; the Church (as means) is sent to bring the salvation of Christ to the world. How then are these two things to meet? Must not the correct conclusion follow from the two premises: Must not the means be judged and measured in the light of the goal? Since "Adam" (that is, since the beginning of creation) and all the more since Christ, the world as a whole stands in the light of grace, nature as a whole has supernature as its intrinsic end, whether it wants it or not, knows it or not. Natural knowledge of God, natural religious ethics stand under this secret sign, whose manifest character the Church proclaims and in a mysterious fashion is. Is this not the meaning of the old patristic doctrine of the *logos spermatikos*?

Were we to put this thinking into practice, the chief directions of contemporary intellectual life, the great impulses of modern times could also find a home in Christianity. "The religious element in mankind" stands as a whole unconsciously in the light of grace and redemption; on every religious road man can find the God of grace. This is the christening of the Enlightenment and of liberal theology from Herbert of Cherbury down to the present day. Further: the end of man as spirit in the world is absolute spirit-being, and this transcendental dynamism again has a supernatural end through the self-opening of the inner love of God himself, so that whoever strives constantly can be called an "anonymous Christian". This is the christening of German Idealism, into whose transcendental key even the metaphysical thinking of St. Thomas can be transposed. Again: the cosmos, biologically considered, is in evolution up to man and beyond him; at the critical moment, the Incarnation of God immerses itself in the world process as its supernatural motive force and brings it to the final maturity of *theosis*, which the Greek Fathers already saw as the Omega point; this is to make a home for Darwin, the valid ideas of the monists and Nietzsche's idea and ethics of the superman. And again: the categories of human existence are only to be defined dialectically; there is no reason why the existential process of following Christ (as, for instance, the *Exercises* express it) cannot lend itself to expression in Hegel's categories. Further: why should a Christian truth not be hidden even in the Marxist total-labor process as the return of mankind from its self-alienation and as the transformation of the world and of man by means of technology? And if Marxism demands the self-immolation of the individual to the collective and to its ideal of the future, why can this process, this sacrifice, this anonymity and poverty of the individual not be understood much more profoundly and transfigured by the light of the salvific order in a Christian "theology of work", according to the principle of hope in an eschatological kingdom into which, in any case, the collective effort of mankind must flow? And again: Is it not only through fellow feeling that man truly becomes man? Is it not precisely here that the absolute and the divine shine forth and become understandable to him, as (following Fichte's profound speculation) Feuerbach and the modern personalists Scheler, Ebner, Buber and Jaspers emphasize? One can almost discern the Sermon on the Mount lying behind all this. Does not the Parable of the Good Samaritan (where it is the "heretic" who does the right thing and is put forward as the example) express precisely this "one thing necessary"? Does not

the parable of Judgment Day (Mt 25) say precisely that
even the just are astounded at the judgment ("Lord, when
did we see you hungry, thirsty, naked, in exile, sick, in
prison?") and hence that the just, too, even when they
are actually Christians, are "anonymous Christians" as
genuine fellow men? Here, at last, true humanism is begotten. And finally (to keep this series to a reasonable
length): is Heidegger not correct when he defines man
as openness to Being, whose ethical nature does not re-
side in his being a servant of laws and commandments
but in his ability to heed the call of Being as a whole
in the momentary situation? And since the Holy Spirit
of God and of Christ holds sway in the All, why should
this essentially mysterious call blowing hither out of the
absolute not be kindled in its depths by the command of
the personal God of love—anonymously, of course—so
that the waters of baptism can be poured out even over
Heidegger's thought?

If we survey all this and comprehend it as a unified
whole, does there not lie in the many ramifications of
this single doctrine a great liberation for Christians of our
time? It rescues us, does it not, from the narrow ecclesi-
asticism that has become incomprehensible in its positive
legalism, and reestablishes our solidarity with all men in
such a way, indeed, that the real law, under which everyone stands, is known by the Christians, who are permitted to announce to the others what they truly are:
beloved children of the Father in Jesus Christ. No wonder that this wholesale method of supernaturalizing what
is worldly (insofar as it is not sinful) today achieves such
colossal success, and that everyone now speaks of "theologies" (of work, of evolution, of the earthly realities, of
the ethical situation, and so forth) where in the first in-

stance simply a "philosophy" might have been expected. No wonder, too, that everyone shows up, closes ranks and marches along: it is plainly the path worn smooth by the vast crowd of travellers, which, even phenomenologically, must be designated "the broad way". The breadth of the cosmic outlook native to the Greek Fathers and even to Thomas Aquinas appears to have been recaptured here on a higher plane. The connection with the culture of the time, after a period of "inner emigration", seems to have been rediscovered. And everything ecclesiastical and positive appears transparent to the universal laws of man and cosmos—and thereby justified. The "worldly office of the Christian" seems assured; the realm of the laity (for which thinkers like Ernst Michel have so long struggled) at last established as the authentic Christian realm. Dark shadows, however, fall on what was previously enclosed and "cloistered": much of this was flight from the world, not to say outright fear and condemnation of it, even Manichaeism. Even the "structures of the Church" (not only her outer "bastions") appear in their instrumentality and relativity; and finally, after a centuries-old ice age, confessional differences miraculously dissolve, awakening hopes where scarcely any existed before. Christians and Christians, Christians and Jews, Christians and non-Christians, Christians and anti-Christians: all commune at last in the great realm of God's creation, which as a whole is endowed with a dimension of grace. Grandiose. But it has a snag. When everything goes so well with anonymity, it is hard to see why a person should still be a name-bearing Christian. And it certainly seems that on the basis if this new theological vogue, πολλοί [the many] (with the best conscience) are already prepared—perhaps out of solidarity with the Russians and Chinese and in order to become an unacknowledged leaven from within—to renounce the troublesome formality of the name.

To my misfortune, however, I had read Kierkegaard in my youth, when he was so popular (Guardini had expounded him to us in Berlin), and there I learned that the apostle of Christ is one who lets himself be killed for Christ. And who today does not lay claim to the title of "apostle"? In the same way as for Kierkegaard, Paul bears the stigmata of the historical Jesus on his body and desires only to live and die for him who loved him and gave himself up for him. If this is our model, then there is no such thing as an anonymous Christian, no matter how many other men—hopefully all!—attain salvation through the grace of Christ. But the grace for all depends on the form of life of him who through the shame of his poverty, his obedience and his bodily "castratedness" (Mt 19:12) embodied God's grace and desired at every stage (Mary; the Apostles; the women in Bethany, at the Cross, at the tomb) that others also partake of this form. Far from being one among many equally important "eschatological signs" for the general public, as is said today in a pacifying tone of voice, this form of life is rather the archetype of all Christian existence, which as such is grounded in the process of dying with Christ to the old world (Rom 6). This form of life is the "salt" of the earth that must not become insipid, and only this form can penetrate the "secular world" as "leaven", since it means standing in the last place in foolishness, weakness and contempt and slander, as the "manure heap of the world", the "latrine for all" (1 Cor 4:10–13).

For this reason, lest everything in the Church become

superficial and insipid, the true, undiminished program for the Church today must read: the greatest possible radiance in the world by virtue of the closest possible following of Christ. At the point where the tension between being a Christian and being a man like other men is at its strongest, indeed so strong that it must appear to the natural man as lacerating and "psychologically" unbearable by every standard of closed and harmonious humanity, there is raised up not only the outer "eschatological" (that is, world-vanquishing) sign—a kind of stimulating irritant—but also the reality itself, either in its visibility or (as with everything weighty in Christianity) in its invisibility. Today this form of existence takes a new ecclesial shape in the "secular institutes". For these as a structure are beyond doubt the unifying midpoint of the Church; they constitute the link between the lay state and the life of the vows and show not only the existential unity of the Church but also her perennial and most "up-to-date" mission in the world.

About this nucleus my activities as author, editor and publisher are gathered in concentric circles. My goal has been to order the treasures of revelation, of Church theology and spirituality critically around this center, bound as much to the past as to the future. This task involves, above all, the administration of the vast literary estate of Adrienne von Speyr, of which some thirty volumes have already been published, with some of the most important still awaiting publication. The collection *Der neue Weg. Schriftenreihe für Weltgemeinschaften* (The new way), which has recently begun, is likewise intended to serve this task. It will discuss the theological, spiritual, canonical, historical and other problems of the new forms of life; the earlier programmatic book *Der Laie und der Ordensstand*

(The laity and the religious state),[12] in a new and more up-to-date version, will be given its place in this series. This task is also served by the essays "Zur Theologie der Säkularinstitute" (On the theology of the secular institute) and, locating them in the living structure of the entire Church, "Zur Theologie des Rätestandes" (A theology of the evangelical counsels).[13] The express theological foundation of the institute was supplied first in the context of contemporary ecclesial thinking in *Wer ist ein Christ? (Who Is a Christian?)*[14] and, more profoundly, in the reconsideration of the problem of form in traditional theology as a whole in *Glaubhaft ist nur Liebe (Love Alone: The Way of Revelation)*.[15] This last synthesis of many earlier efforts to express the meaning and form of theology sought to serve both as an exposition of Christian revelation and as a guide to Christian proclamation and ethics by displaying the gospel event before our era as directly and abruptly as possible. The simpler and clearer the fathomless depth of God's love becomes to us, indeed, the

[12] Einsiedeln: Johannes Verlag; 5th ed., 1989.

[13] "Zur Theologie der Säkularinstitute", in *Geist und Leben* 29:182–205. Included in *Sponsa Verbi*. Skizzen zur Theologie 2 (Einsiedeln: Johannes Verlag, 1960; 2d ed., 1971); English translation: *Church and World* (New York: Herder and Herder, 1967). New edition, "Towards a Theology of the Secular Institute" in *Spouse of the Word*. Explorations in Theology 2 (San Francisco: Ignatius Press, 1991). "Zur Theologie des Rätestandes", in: Stephan Richter, O.F.M. (ed.), *Wagnis der Nachfolge* (Paderborn: Schöningh, 1964), 9–57; English translation: "A Theology of the Evangelical Counsels", in: *Cross Currents* (1966).

[14] *Wer ist ein Christ?* (Einsiedeln: Benziger, 1965; 4th ed., Einsiedeln: Johannes Verlag, 1983). English translation: *Who Is a Christian?* (Westminster, Md.: Newman Press, 1968).

[15] *Glaubhaft ist nur Liebe*, Christ heute 5/1 (Einsiedeln: Johannes Verlag, 1963; 5th ed., 1985). English translation: *Love Alone: The Way of Revelation* (London: Sheed and Ward, 1968).

more incomprehensible to us the thought becomes that, in the face of such a mystery, man could be capable of something like correspondence and following at all, the sooner will we be rid of the distorted and simplistic thinking that makes the Christian message so unbelievable today. By the same token ecumenical dialogue can bear fruit only if it seizes on what is most deeply Christian and, faithful to its utter seriousness, develops a sense for what is secondary and relative, for what therefore can be conceded on both sides.

2. Rays from the Center

If what we have just written provides an initial description of the existential center for the Christian, the real theological center, from which the world of creation and of history receives its structures, is occupied not by the Christian but by Christ. *Theologie der Geschichte (A Theology of History)* [16] begins by pointing exclusively to Christ's form of existence at the center of history, where the time of sin and reprobation is reintegrated into God's original time by virtue of Christ's pure loving obedience to the Father. This earthly obedience has as its terminus the Father's coming "hour", which the Son awaits even while subjecting himself to the creaturely time common to all men, so that in this attitude he becomes the measure and norm of every temporal existence. Biblically and theologically it is not illegitimate—indeed, for the following of Christ it is important—to see the fundamental act of Christ's existence as the archetypal act of faith, in whose

[16] *Theologie der Geschichte*, Christ heute 1/8 (Einsiedeln: Johannes Verlag, 1959; 6th ed., 1979). English translation: *A Theology of History* (New York: Sheed and Ward, 1963).

expanse the possibility of the Church's faith is first and foremost established (cf. "Fides Christi").[17]

This nucleus of a theology of history was developed in its universal historical dimensions in *Das Ganze im Fragment (A Theological Anthropology)*.[18] Beginning with an Augustinian consideration of "distancing" (*diastasis*) between a pure time of love and a time of sin, this work treats the perfectability both of mortal man and of history as a whole, ending with a sketch of a christological reintegration of man's fragmentary and concrete "stages of life" into their final eschatological form. The emphasis is on the latter; such a notion of integration is the basis for my mistrust of every simplistic, straight-line evolutionism in past and present, as discussed in my article on the spirituality of Teilhard de Chardin (1963).[19]

What *Das Ganze im Fragment* treats as a whole is separated into its individual aspects in the first volume of my collected essays, *Verbum Caro*.[20] The conditions that revelation presupposes for the above-mentioned integra-

[17] "Fides Christi", in: *Sponsa Verbi*. English translation: "*Fides Christi*: An Essay on the Consciousness of Christ" in *The Spouse of the Word*. Explorations in Theology 2 (San Francisco: Ignatius Press, 1991).

[18] *Das Ganze im Fragment. Aspekte der Geschichtstheologie* (Einsiedeln: Benziger, 1963; 2d ed., Einsiedeln: Johannes Verlag, 1989). English translation: *A Theological Anthropology* (New York: Sheed and Ward, 1967); and *Man in History: A Theological Study* (London: Sheed and Ward, 1968).

[19] In: *Wort und Wahrheit* 18:339–50.

[20] *Verbum Caro*. Skizzen zur Theologie 1 (Einsiedeln: Johannes Verlag, 1960; 2d ed., 1965). English translation: in two volumes: *Word and Revelation*, Essays in Theology 1 (New York: Herder and Herder, 1964), and *Word and Redemption*, Essays in Theology 2 (New York: Herder and Herder, 1965); new edition: *The Word Made Flesh*. Explorations in Theology 1 (San Francisco: Ignatius Press, 1989).

tion of man to God through Christ are portrayed in the
sketch "God Speaks as Man", where human nature in all
its forms is understood as the essential language of the
Logos. In like manner, "The Implications of the Word"
shows the inescapability of human thinking and philosophizing as a presupposition for God's speaking ("revelation") and being understood ("theology"). Vis-à-vis
Karl Barth, who is the real dialogue partner in this book
because he, like no other Protestant, was concerned with
this tension between the Christ-center and the universal-
ity of salvation, I argued that the Christian "exclusivity"
demands precisely the inclusion of all human thinking:
as something judged [*gerichtetes*], it is "broken", realigned
and reset [*ab- aus-, und eingerichtet*]. "Some Points of Eschatology" draws the consequences from *Theologie der
Geschichte*,[21] when it relates the last "things" to the last
(that is, ultimate) "person" Jesus Christ as to the freely
judging measure and norm: a first draft that, if God allows, will be followed by a detailed theology of hell as a
commentary to still unpublished works of Adrienne von
Speyr on the theology of Holy Saturday.

One stage farther back lies the dialogue with Barth. In
Karl Barth (*The Theology of Karl Barth*),[22] the fundamental
reconcilability of Catholic and Protestant theology is described at the point where each is most consistently itself.
For Barth, this means that, despite everything, the truly
evangelical element in Protestantism lies beyond Luther

[21] "Eschatologie", in: J. Feiner, J. Trütsch and F. Böckle (eds.), *Fragen
der Theologie heute* (Einsiedeln: Benziger, 1957), 403–21.

[22] *Karl Barth. Darstellung und Deutung seiner Theologie* (Cologne and
Olten: Hegner, 1951; 4th ed., Einsiedeln: Johannes Verlag, 1976). English translation: *The Theology of Karl Barth* (San Francisco: Ignatius Press,
1992).

(and all the more beyond Calvin) in Schleiermacher: in the opening of the concrete universal that is Christ to the world-embracing *Logos*. For the Catholic, it means that the concept of nature that Catholic theology is accustomed to presuppose undialectically can in reality only be grasped dialectically, in accord with Henri de Lubac's renewed vision of patristic-high-scholastic theology. If unity is once achieved at this depth, then in principle everything else is open for ecumenical discussion. Hans Küng continued this discussion, taking it on beyond fundamental theology into the sphere of dogmatics (the doctrine of justification), and here Barth indicated his agreement in principle.

3. A Church of Disciples

The next circle of themes necessarily extends beyond those treated above. The second volume of my collected essays, *Sponsa Verbi*,[23] published in English as *Spouse of the Word*, Exploration in Theology 2, asks explicitly: "Who is the Church?" According to the answer given, the Church in her deepest reality is the unity of those who, gathered and formed by the immaculate and therefore limitless assent of Mary, which through grace has the form of Christ, are prepared to let the saving will of God take place in themselves and for all their brothers. This primordial act is what is meant by "hearing the Word"; it justifies and demands contemplative prayer (as described in *Das betrachtende Gebet* (*Prayer*),[24] not in the mere Greek sense

---

[23] *Sponsa Verbi*. English translation: *Spouse of the Word*. Explorations in Theology 2.

[24] *Das betrachtende Gebet* (Einsiedeln: Johannes Verlag, 1955; 4th ed., 1977). English translation: *Prayer* (New York: Sheed and Ward, 1961;

of the word, but normatively in the biblical sense of the whole man's openness in faith to the ever-greater meaning of the word of God. It justifies, likewise, the preparatory opening up of Scripture to this act, as in my meditations on the Thessalonian and Pastoral Epistles. It justifies, precisely for our time, a life of sacrificial surrender to God's word, as contemplatives live it in service to God for the salvation of all the world. An example of the latter was given in *Therese von Lisieux, Geschichte einer Sendung* (*Thérèse of Lisieux. The Story of a Mission*),[25] where the discussion turns on the saint's understanding of Carmel as the highest bridal fruitfulness for the Church. In *Elisabeth von Dijon* (*Elizabeth of the Trinity*),[26] this is completed by the latter contemplative's interpretation of her existence according to the Pauline formula "in praise of God's glory". Precisely Elizabeth, who understood the glory for which she lived (*doxa, gloria*) as both the exclusivity of crucified love and the absolute inclusivity of universal salvation, reveals clearly once again how the Protestantism of Barth agrees with the innermost mys-

---

New York: Paulist Press, 1967; new English translation: San Francisco: Ignatius Press, 1986).

[25] *Therese von Lisieux. Geschichte einer Sendung* (Cologne and Olten: Hegner-Bücherei, 1950; Einsiedeln: Johannes Verlag, 1970). English translation: *Thérèse of Lisieux. The Story of a Mission* (New York: Sheed and Ward, 1954). Together with *Elisabeth von Dijon und ihre geistliche Sendung* in: *Schwestern im Geist. Therese von Lisieux und Elisabeth von Dijon*, 4th ed. (1990). New English translation: *Two Sisters in the Spirit* (San Francisco: Ignatius Press, 1992).

[26] *Elisabeth von Dijon und ihre geistliche Sendung* (Cologne and Olten: Hegner-Bücherei, 1952). English translation: *Elizabeth of Dijon: An Interpretation of Her Spiritual Mission* (New York: Pantheon, 1956). Cf. n. 25, above. New edition: *Elizabeth of the Trinity* in *Two Sisters in the Spirit*.

tery of Catholicism. The penetrating power of Thérèse and Charles de Foucauld (whose mission I also treated)[27] shows, even in this era of anti-contemplative lay ideologies, how right they and their kind really are.

Wherever and to whatever extent this fundamental act of hearing the word takes place (as faith, love, obedience, bridal fidelity), there is the spiritual Church. Wherever this is lacking, the Church becomes herself the "whore Jerusalem", as discussed in the lengthy article "Casta Meretrix".[28] Reception of the word by the whole man, body and soul, requires a unity of word and sacrament, as described in "Seeing, Believing, Eating".[29] The institutional aspects of the Church exist for the sake of this act and receive their intelligible form from it (cf. "Office in the Church" and "Priestly Existence").[30] It is at this point, too, that the dialogue between Church and synagogue—theologically and existentially so opaque and burdened by past history—takes place: like Barth, Przywara, Journet and Fessard before me, I attempted to situate it for both parties in the Pauline radicality of Romans 9–11, in Einsame Zwiesprach. Martin Buber und das Christentum (Martin Buber and Christianity)[31] especially and, more generally, elsewhere. The notion of the Church as

[27] Cf. Charles de Foucauld, Der letzte Platz. Sigillum Collection 8 (Einsiedeln: Johannes Verlag, 1957; 7th ed., 1979).

[28] "Casta Meretrix", in: Sponsa Verbi. English translation: Spouse of the Word. Explorations in Theology 2.

[29] Ibid.

[30] Ibid.

[31] Einsame Zwiesprache. Martin Buber und das Christentum (Cologne and Olten: Hegner-Bücherei, 1958). English translation: Martin Buber and Christianity: A Dialogue between Israel and the Church (New York: Macmillan, 1961).

"chaste whore" makes such a dialogue doubly confusing and humiliating for the Christian.

From the standpoint of Marian and ecclesial spirituality (which is one with loving and hoping faith), it is both legitimate and necessary to examine the interpretation of this fullness in the endless variety of specialized "charisms", "missions", or "spiritualities". The inseparable unity of "Charis and Charisma",[32] that is, of sanctifying grace and the task of sanctification, was first asserted against the (only partially defensible) tradition to the contrary in an extensive commentary on St. Thomas' tractate, *Summa Theologica* II–II, 171–82, on charisms.[33] This commentary treats historically and critically the three theological *loci* of such phenomena: namely, Old and New Testament prophecy, the gifts of the Holy Spirit as supernatural and experiential perfection of the Christian virtues and the interrelationship between contemplation and action. These three are opened out and set into relationship to one another. In addition, beginning with my translation into German of Augustine's treatise on prophecy and vision,[34] I undertook numerous editorial and critical tasks intended to bring to the attention of our all-forgetting era the richness of the ancient Christian and medieval vistas, a task that far exceeds the power of a single editor or publisher. An entire team would be

---

[32] In *Sponsa Verbi*. English translation: *Spouse of the Word*. Explorations in Theology 2.

[33] Volume 12 of the German-Latin edition of Thomas: *Besondere Gnadengaben und die zwei Wege menschlichen Lebens* (F. H. Kerle-A. Pustet, 1954).

[34] Augustine, *Psychologie und Mystik*, translation and introduction together with M. E. Korger. Sigillum Collection 18 (Einsiedeln: Johannes Verlag, 1960).

needed. The three series *Menschen der Kirche* (Men of the Church), *Lectio Spiritualis* and *Sigillum* are only a makeshift stop-gap that attempts to sift and winnow the contents of the tradition in such a way that even today's reader can grasp that it is essential and, indeed, indispensable. The wealth of names, the points of view governing the selection, can neither be listed nor defended here in individual detail; chief figures emerge to dominate the whole: above all, Irenaeus,[35] Origen, in a selection of over one thousand texts presented in the fundamental structure of his thought: *Origenes, Geist und Feuer* (*Origen: Spirit and Fire*)[36] and *Parole et Mystère chez Origène* (Word and mystery in Origen),[37] Gregory of Nyssa, *Présence et Pensée, Essai sur la philosophie religieuse de Grégoire de Nysse* (Presence and thought: Essay on the religious philosophy of Gregory of Nyssa),[38] a sketch of the whole, entitled *Der versiegelte Quell* (The sealed fountain),[39] Dionysius the Areopagite,[40] Maximus[41] and naturally a selection from

---

[35] Irenäus, *Geduld des Reifens. Die christliche Antwort auf den gnostischen Mythos des 2. Jahrhunderts*, Klosterberg Collection (Basel: Schwabe, 1943). 2d improved ed.: Sigillum Collection 6 (Einsiedeln: Johannes Verlag, 1956). New ed.: *Gott in Fleisch und Blut. Ein Durchblick in Texten*, Christliche Meister Collection 11, with revised introduction (Einsiedeln: Johannes Verlag, 1982). English translation: *The Scandal of the Incarnation: Irenaeus against the Heresies*, selected and with an introduction by Hans Urs von Balthasar (San Francisco: Ignatius Press, 1990).

[36] See n. 2 above.

[37] Ibid.

[38] Ibid.

[39] Ibid.

[40] Dionysius the Areopagite, *Von den Namen zum Unnenbaren*, selected and introduced by Endre von Ivánka, Sigillum Collection 7 (Einsiedeln: Johannes Verlag, 1957); new ed. in: Christliche Meister Collection 39 (Einsiedeln: Johannes Verlag, 1990).

[41] *Kosmische Liturgie.*

Augustine's commentary on the Psalms,[42] the theology of
the homiletic works in *Das Antlitz der Kirche* (The face of
the Church),[43] introductions to the *Confessions*[44] and to
the *City of God*,[45] then Anselm, William of St. Thierry,[46]
the two Mechthilds,[47] the great English mystical tradition
(Julian,[48] the Cloud,[49] Hilton, a volume of Richard Rolle
is planned), while ample provision has been made else-

---

[42] Augustine, *Über die Psalmen* (Leipzig: Hegner, 1936); 2d ed., Christliche Meister Collection 20 (Einsiedeln: Johannes Verlag, 1983).

[43] Augustine, *Das Antlitz der Kirche. Auswahl und Einleitung*. Menschen
der Kirche in Zeugnis und Urkunde (Einsiedeln: Benziger, 1942; 2d
ed., 1955).

[44] Fischer-Bücherei, 1955. My own translation with a new introduction: *Die Bekenntnisse*, Christliche Meister Collection 25 (Einsiedeln:
Johannes Verlag, 1985; 2d ed., 1988).

[45] Augustine, *Die Gottesbürgerschaft. De Civitate Dei* (Fischer-Bücherei,
1961); *Der Gottesstaat*, Christliche Meister Collection 16 (Einsiedeln:
Johannes Verlag, 1982).

[46] William of St. Thierry, *Gott schauen und Gott lieben* (*Tractatus de con-
templando Deo; Tractatus de natura et dignitate amoris*), translated and introduced together with Frau Winfrida Dittrich, O.S.B., Sigillum Collection 21 (Einsiedeln: Johannes Verlag, 1961); included in *Spiegel des
Glaubens*, Christliche Meister Collection 12 (Einsiedeln: Johannes Verlag, 1981).

[47] Mechthild von Hackeborn, *Das Buch von strömenden Lob (Liber spe-
cialis Gratiae)*. Selection, translation, introduction. Sigillum Collection
4 (Einsiedeln: Johannes Verlag, 1955; 2d ed., 1987); also in: Christliche
Meister Collection 36. Introduction to Mechthild von Magdeburg, *Das
fliessende Licht der Gottheit*, Menschen der Kirche NF 3 (Einsiedeln: Benziger, 1955).

[48] Julian of Norwich, *Offenbarung von göttlicher Liebe*. Translated for
the first time from the original Middle English text and introduced
by Elisabeth Strakosch. Sigillum Collection 17 (Einsiedeln: Johannes
Verlag, 1960; 2d ed., 1988); also in Christliche Meister Collection 36.

[49] *Die Wolke des Nichtwissens: Ein anonymes englisches Werk des 14.
Jahrhunderts*. First German translation by Elisabeth Strakosch. Intro-

where for knowledge of the German mystics. But new access had to be provided to Joan of Arc and Catherine of Siena,[50] John of the Cross in an improved translation, Lallemant[51] and his school were to be called afresh to memory (an edition of Surin is in preparation). And Peter Faber, the first Jesuit in his chosen homeland Germany, has finally come into his own with the childlike prudence of his *Memoriale*,[52] and the *Letters* of his father Ignatius in the marvelous translation and commentary by Hugo Rahner have gone through three editions already. Angelus Silesius[53] had to be rescued from false accusation, the voice of Görres had to be heard in the spiritual choir, and among the more modern voices it was above all the authentic form of the *Autobiographical Writings* of Thérèse of Lisieux[54] that had to be presented in German,

duction by Endre von Ivánka. Sigillum Collection 14 (Einsiedeln: Johannes Verlag, 1958); new ed., ed. Wolfgang Riehle, Christliche Meister Collection 8 (Einsiedeln: Johannes Verlag, 1980).

[50] Catherine of Siena, *Gespräch von Gottes Vorsehung*. Introduction by E. Sommer-von Seckendorff and Hans Urs von Balthasar, Lectio Spiritualis 8 (Einsiedeln: Johannes Verlag, 1963; 3d ed., 1985).

[51] Louis Lallemant, *Geistliche Lehre*, Lectio Spiritualis 8 (Einsiedeln: Johannes Verlag, 1960).

[52] Peter Faber, *Memoriale. Das geistliche Tagebuch des ersten Jesuiten in Deutschland*, translated from the manuscripts with introduction by Peter Henrici, S.J., Lectio Spiritualis 5 (Einsiedeln: Johannes Verlag, 1963); 2d ed., Christliche Meister Collection 38 (1989).

[53] Angelus Silesius, *Dich auftun wie die Rose*, selection from the *Cherubinischer Wandersmann* with postscript. Sigillum Collection 3 (Einsiedeln: Johannes Verlag, 1954); 2d ed., Christliche Meister Collection 6 (1980; 3d ed., 1984).

[54] Thérèse of the Child Jesus, *Selbstbiographische Schriften*, for the first time in the original text. Lectio Spiritualis 1 (Einsiedeln: Johannes Verlag, 1958; 8th ed. in paperback, 1978; 11th ed., 1988).

while close beside these it was necessary to set a translation of the unique document of a philosophy that came
into being in an intimate dialogue with God: Maurice
Blondel's *Carnets Intimes* (German translation: *Tagebuch
vor Gott*), written during the laborious composition of
his chief work *L'Action*.[55] And Divo Barsotti's burning
dialectic of the heart had to be included.[56]

Priority belonged to *Die grossen Ordensregeln* (The great
religious orders),[57] because here the speakers are not
merely individuals but the founders of the great directions of Catholic spirituality. Here I could begin with a
discussion of the religious state in general.[58] In the section
that was my special task, the Rule of Basil, I dealt with the
essential original relationship between the gospel and the
group of those in the community who knew themselves
to be called to represent its genuine form; much on this
subject is stated at a deeper level in the second edition of
this book.

If all these undertakings add up only to a paltry selection from the inexhaustible plenitude of holiness that
the Holy Spirit continues to draw from the evangelical
source, Adrienne von Speyr's remarkable book on the
prayer life of the saints will fill this out immensely. In
any event, this fullness will only appear richer and richer

[55] Maurice Blondel, *Tagebuch vor Gott*, with introduction by Peter
Henrici, S.J. (Einsiedeln: Johannes Verlag, 1964; 2d ed., 1988).

[56] Divo Barsotti, *Die regungslose Flucht. Geistliches Tagebuch*, Lectio
Spiritualis 2 (Einsiedeln: Johannes Verlag, 1960).

[57] *Die grossen Ordensregeln: Basilius, Augustinus, Benedikt, Franziskus, Ig-
natius von Loyola*, with introduction. Menschen der Kirche (Einsiedeln:
Benziger, 1947); new ed., with many revisions (1961); 3d ed., Lectio
Spiritualis 12 (Einsiedeln: Johannes Verlag, 1974; 6th ed., 1988).

[58] Cf. introduction to *Die grossen Ordensregeln*.

as time goes on. Yet what it always involves is a proportion between the archetype and the copy, which permits us to treat "Das Evangelium als kritische Norm für jede Form kirchlicher Spiritualität" (The gospel as critical norm for every form of spirituality in the Church)[59] and, among other things, to win a superior criterion for judging the new forms of Christian spirituality that announce themselves in the radical changes of the present.

With this norm in view, a few chief ideas can be selected: the Christian lives from the strength of Christ's grace; his living faith is essentially "infused virtue"; his mission, whether it succeed or miscarry, is answered for by Christ's word of commission. Thus the mission, not the psychology of the saints, must always have the last word, even with—indeed, precisely with—the famous "subjectivists" (Augustine, Pascal, Kierkegaard, Dostoyevsky, and so on), as my article in the *Schweizer Rundschau*,[60] questioning the notion of the psychology of the saints, points out. In reality, these individuals live by virtue of what on a philosophical plane Sciacca has called "objective interiority".[61] Augustine, in particular, was interpreted in this sense,[62] while Thérèse's *Story of a Soul* was

[59] "Das Evangelium als kritische Norm für jede Form kirchlicher Spiritualität", in *Concilium* 1:715–22. In *Spiritus Creator*. Skizzen zur Theologie 3 (Einsiedeln: Johannes Verlag, 1967). English translation: "The Gospel as Norm and Critique of All" in *Creator Spirit*. Explorations in Theology 3 (San Francisco: Ignatius Press, 1993).

[60] In: *Schweizer Rundschau* 48:644–53.

[61] Michele Federico Sciacca, *Objektive Innerlichkeit*, translated from Italian by Karl Huber. Horizonte Collection 10 (Einsiedeln: Johannes Verlag, 1965).

[62] Augustine, in: *Herrlichkeit. Eine theologische Ästhetik*, vol. 2: *Fächer der Stile*, part 1: *Klerikale Stile* (Einsiedeln: Johannes Verlag, 1962; 3d ed., 1984). English translation: *The Glory of the Lord: A Theological Aes-*

interpreted as *Story of a Mission*,[63] and the writers Georges
Bernanos[64] and Reinhold Schneider[65] were treated likewise in a pair of extensive monographs.

Bernanos, the deeply suffering Christian, who could
often appear as an almost lawless *Pneumatiker*, in truth
simply exposed himself in terrifying nakedness of soul to
the evangelical fire, as to a brand that, for the poet, is
applied only by the sacramental torches the Church kin-
dles. The torch of baptism is treated in *Une Nuit* (*One
Night*);[66] holy orders and the Eucharist, confession and
anointing in *Sous le soleil de Satan* (*The Star of Satan*), *Apostates* (*Apostates*), *La Joie* (*Joy*), and the *Journal d'un curé de
campagne* (*Diary of a Country Priest*); the objective, quasi-
sacramental power of the vows in *Dialogues des Carmelites*
(*The Carmelites*).[67] And if the poet lived in an abysmal
anguish, he understood how to assimilate this anguish
ultimately to the anguish of Gethsemane, far beyond the
philosophical dread of Heidegger and the slightly neu-
rotic anxiety of Kierkegaard; genuine Christian anguish

---

thetics, vol. 2: *Studies in Theological Style: Clerical Styles* (San Francisco:
Ignatius Press, New York: Crossroad, 1984).

[63] *Therese von Lisieux. Geschichte einer Sendung.* English translation: *Two
Sisters in the Spirit* (San Francisco: Ignatius Press, 1992).

[64] Under the title *Gelebte Kirche: Bernanos* (Cologne and Olten: Hegner-Bücherei, 1954; 3d ed., 1988). French translation by M. de Gandil-
lac (Paris: Éditions du Seuil, 1955; 2d ed., n.d.).

[65] *Reinhold Schneider. Sein Leben und sein Werk* (Cologne and Olten:
Hegner-Bücherei, 1953). 2d revised and expanded edition (Einsiedeln,
Johannes Verlag), in preparation.

[66] Georges Bernanos, *Eine Nacht, Novellen*, translated with postscript.
Christ heute 3/5 (Einsiedeln: Johannes Verlag, 1954; 2d ed., Stuttgart:
Reclam, 1961).

[67] Georges Bernanos, *Die begnadete Angst* (Freiburg: Herder-Bücherei
[vol. 48], 1959).

is the putrefaction of sin at last transposed into consuming fire. In my little book on anxiety and the Christian, *Der Christ und die Angst* (*The Christian and anxiety*),[68] I had already attempted to relate an important symptom of modern existence to biblical categories, and here the seventeenth chapter of the Book of Wisdom appeared particularly illuminating. On two subsequent occasions, without regard to Bernanos, the Bible had brought me close to his world of feeling: once in preparing the text for a series of monotypes by Hans Fronius on *König David* (*King David*):[69] these stories from the Book of Kings have their place alongside the old Greek sagas of Titans and heroes and the German sagas of the *Nibelungen*. A second time in preparing the text for the late Hegenbarth's *Kreuzweg* (*Way of the Cross*),[70] where, just as the painter freely and responsibly had renounced his brilliance in order to descend with the Lord into the *kenosis* of all beauty (an impenetrable mystery of Christian art), the words, too, had to be broken and rendered helpless in order to approximate an objective form of anguish that might serve only the unique anguish of the wholly Other.

Reinhold Schneider was a tragic Aeolian harp that later truly broke and emitted only confused sounds, instead of precise notes (see his *Winter in Wien*), sounds that appear interesting to those of a decadent turn of mind but that ob-

---

[68] *Der Christ und die Angst* (Einsiedeln: Johannes Verlag, 1951; 6th ed., 1989).

[69] *König David.* Text with illustrations by Hans Fronius (Einsiedeln: Johannes Verlag, 1955).

[70] Josef Hegenbarth and Hans Urs von Balthasar, *Der Kreuzweg in der St.-Hedwigs-Kathedrale in Berlin* (Mainz: Matthias-Grünewald-Verlag, 1964). English translation: *The Way of the Cross* (New York: Herder and Herder, 1969).

scured the genuinely prophetic quality of his great works. He lived, in conscious opposition to his own age, on the basis of an anti-psychological ethos of service and of the representation of a divine-kingly order. Certainly (as Max Müller has shown), this is an order in the void, a construction erected against the background of chaos, and so this island of Christianity was continually threatened by the raging Buddhist-Schopenhauerian waves. And yet, what power the vision had, when it was a question of confronting in naked antithesis the Christian mission of the holiness that involves renunciation and the secular commission of princely governance with power! What sublimity in the way the problem was posed, in the description of the lacerating dialectic between both realms, in the tragic mutual self-destruction, when one compares Schneider's historical dramas and epic frescoes, the lightning flashes of his short stories, the iron tones of his sonnets, with the insipid chatter that is so common among theologians today about the modern Christian's task in the world! Indeed, who else has so described, even formally, the tension, referred to above, that exists between gospel and world? Who else has demanded so calmly the "heroic" renunciation of the Christian as the one presupposition for effectiveness in the world? And yet he was unable to endure all this so that there was for me no escaping the task of venturing the same thing with other means, amidst other historical and theological omens than those attending this lonely, tragic wreckage of a man, who knew about the greatest missions and yet was not fully able to live his own without the secret self-righteousness of the overburdened Job. Surely this is a warning and a pointer to the inner form of the secular institutes. And later, when engaged on a renewed study of Greek tragedy, there grew the certainty, which Schneider shared, that the decisive dialogue between antiquity and Christianity lay not so much in the centuries-old exchange between Plato and patristic-scholastic theology as in that between the Greek tragedians and the Christian saints about the meaning of human existence. I have discussed this in my article on tragedy and Christian faith.[71]

Mere renunciation of the world cannot be tragic, but only the struggle for the proper love of the world in God, for an affirmation that, intersected by the Cross, does not separate Creator and creature. In my early period, this affirmation bore the names of Goethe, Jean Paul and Nietzsche;[72] Derleth's *Fränkischer Koran*[73] appeared as a fulfillment; it is sheer joy for me that I was later permitted to publish Rolf Schott's poems:[74] he utters this Christian-secular affirmation with a deeper discernment of spirits than Derleth. In this regard, all else was soon drowned by the powerful organ peal of Paul Claudel. After translating *Soulier de satin* (*The Satin Slipper*) in the thirties, I proceeded to render into German the many volumes of his collected poetry, a task that stretched over more than twenty-five years. The lyrical mountain chain of his poetry continued unbroken, even if next to the com-

---

[71] In: *Hochland* 57:497–510, and in: *Spiritus Creator*. Skizzen zur Theologie 3 ("Die Tragödie und der christliche Glaube") (Einsiedeln: Johannes Verlag, 1967). English translation: "Tragedy and Christian Faith" in *Creator Spirit*. Explorations in Theology 3.

[72] *Apokalypse der deutschen Seele.*

[73] Ibid.

[74] Rolf Schott, *Orbis pictus*. Klosterberg Collection (Basel: Schwabe, 1946); *Lebensbaum. Gedichte*, Christ heute 4/9 (Einsiedeln: Johannes Verlag, 1958); and *Ein Glanz aus Dir. Zum Geleit* (Einsiedeln: Johannes Verlag, 1965).

plete successes (*Cinq grandes odes, La Cantate à trois voix*,[75] "L'Architecte",[76] "Saint Thérèse", "Ode jubilaire pour le six-centième anniversaire de la mort de Dante", "Introït", *La Messe la-bas*,[77] and many others) there were also some mediocre, forced efforts, although only rarely complete failures and never anything talentless. Like his hero Roderigo, like his nearest of kin Dante, the everywhere alien and homeless Claudel was able to breathe only in the entirety of the world and hence to live only in a love whose horizons are the world, embracing hell and Purgatory and paradise at once: in the spacious kingdom of Doña Musique, who can rule even beyond the tragic strife dividing the celestial and subterranean Muses, who is at once the simile of the world in its inherent (created and redeemed) goodness and the symbol of the West, whose Christian dome is erected once and for all on the foundations of antiquity—"*Santa Maria sopra Minerva*", as Karl Barth mockingly said and as Claudel would have repeated affirmatively from the bottom of his heart. With my translation of *L'Annonce faite à Marie*,[78] the limitations

[75] *Fünf grosse Oden*, see: Paul Claudel, *Fünf grosse Oden* (Freiburg: Herder, 1939; 3d ed., Einsiedeln: Johannes Verlag, 1964). Cf. also *Gesammelte Werke*, vol. 1: *Lyrik* (Einsiedeln: Benziger; Heidelberg: F. H. Kerle, 1963). For *Singspiel*: see Paul Claudel, *Verse der Verbannung/ Singspiel für drei Stimmen* (Einsiedeln: Johannes Verlag, 1964). Cf. also *Gesammelte Werke*, vol. 1: *Lyrik*.

[76] *Der Architekt, Die Heilige Theresia* and *Dantehymnus*, in: Paul Claudel, *Heiligenblätter* (Einsiedeln: Johannes Verlag, 1964). Cf. also *Gesammelte Werke*, vol. 1: *Lyrik*.

[77] Paul Claudel, *Die Messe fernab*. In: *Gesammelte Werke*, vol. 1: *Gedichte* (Einsiedeln-Zurich-Cologne: Benziger and Heidelberg: Kerle, 1963). Cf. *Die Messe des Verbannten*, Christliche Meister Collection 13 (Einsiedeln: Johannes Verlag, 1981).

[78] Paul Claudel, *Mariä Verkündigung* (Lucerne: Stocker, 1943).

of the young Claudel, still heavily dependent on symbolism and *Jugendstil*, became clear; it gathered dust in a way that never happened with *The Satin Slipper*.

Next to Claudel and of almost equal rank with him is Péguy: still a Christian in the tension between gospel and world, one who for the sake of brotherly love left the Church and for the sake of brotherly love returned to her again. His *Le Porche du mystère de la deuxième vertu*,[79] which I translated into German, is a basic Christian text no less than his other two *Mystères* which I would dearly like to translate too. Only a small representative selection of his prose has been translated,[80] but in volume 2, part 2, of *Herrlichkeit* (*The Glory of the Lord*, volume 3)[81] Péguy has the task of providing a valid representation of twentieth-century Catholicism: for he understood fully the face-to-face encounter between Greek tragedy and Christian martyrdom (in the *Note Conjointe*).[82] With him, however, the sphere of the world is not so much *physis*, as with Claudel; rather it is the un-Christian or anti-Christian communist brother. Joan of Arc, who begins in the most serious commitment for the world and ends in the flames of the Cross, is for Péguy the beloved embodiment of this ideal. I wonder if the Germans have ever really learned to

[79] Charles Péguy, *Das Tor zum Geheimnis der Hoffnung* (Lucerne: Stocker, 1943; 2d revised ed., Einsiedeln: Johannes Verlag, 1980).

[80] Charles Péguy, *Wir stehen alle an der Front*. Selection from his prose, with introduction. Christ heute 3/3 (Einsiedeln: Johannes Verlag, 1952).

[81] *Herrlichkeit. Eine theologische Ästhetik*, vol. 2: *Fächer der Stile*, part 2: *Laikale Stile* (Einsiedeln: Johannes Verlag, 1962; 3d ed., 1984). English translation: *The Glory of the Lord: A Theological Aesthetics*, vol. 3: *Studies in Theological Style: Lay Styles* (San Francisco: Ignatius Press, 1986).

[82] Charles Péguy, *Notre conjointe. Oeuvres en prose 1909–1914*, Pléiade (Paris: Gallimard, 1957), 1301ff.

listen to Péguy? Perhaps, if one is really to do so, one must be at home on both sides of the river, like my esteemed friend Annette Kolb, or one must have antennae as fine as another friend of mine, Walter Warnach. There is no special merit in the position of the Swiss, who stands on the bridge.

One more name must be included here: that of the Catholic artist and pilgrim to Greece Richard Seewald, with whom years ago I collaborated on a collection of texts and illustrations for the Christian year, *Das Christliche Jahr* (The Christian year).[83] We have both travelled a long way since that time. My volume of scholarly portraits describing the seminal thinkers and artists of Western civilization (*Herrlichkeit* 3/1 [*The Glory of the Lord* 4 and 5])[84] is of a piece with the Occident that he has portrayed in the halls of the Munich *Hofgarten*. We both know clearly that we have no resting place here and that our earthly tent, together with the beloved spiritual landscapes that surround it, will in the end be folded up.

The present is continually pressing forward, penetrating into the unknown and forcing new decisions: one senses this if one directs a series with the title *Christ heute* (The Christian today) over the course of several decades, or even only when one meets young people: year by year, day by day, the whole must be seen anew with fresh eyes. While the fullness of the Church's tra-

---

[83] Richard Seewald and Hans Urs von Balthasar, *Das Christliche Jahr.* Text with illustrations by Richard Seewald (Lucerne: Stocker, 1944).

[84] *Herrlichkeit. Eine theologische Ästhetik*, vol. 3/1: *In Raum der Metaphysik*, part 1: *Alterium* (Einsiedeln: Johannes Verlag: 1965; 2d ed., 1975). English translation: *The Glory of the Lord: A Theological Aesthetics*, vol. 4: *The Realm of Metaphysics in Antiquity* (San Francisco: Ignatius Press, 1989).

dition has been my concern, it is only for the sake of preserving what is valuable for the future, since only the best has a chance to survive. On the other hand, it is probably more important to have served this "best" than the obvious ephemera of the present day. Many of the great works of the past have already moved on beyond the questions that to our contemporaries seem completely modern and without precedent. Does it make sense to explain to this modern man what distinguishes his special religious situation from that of previous generations? To a certain degree perhaps. And I have attempted the task in *Die Gottesfrage des heutigen Menschen (The God Question and Modern Man)*,[85] but the results disappointed me. Instead the thought arose of presenting in a somewhat rounded-off form the aspect of Christianity that can no more be outgrown by today's man than it was by men of the past. Thus there came to maturity the plan of a trilogy that I, at any rate, will not complete, since its first Part, the *Theologische Ästhetik*, already fills four stout volumes; the theological *Dramatik* and *Logik* will doubtless wait for me in vain after these volumes. It had, however, to be a sustained piece of work, in order to offer something more unified than the usual "collected tidbits" of a "team" presented in the guise of a "*Festschrift*", "Dogmatics", or "Theological Lexicon". For, unfortunately, a hundred approaches still do not make a single jump, nor a hundred separate castings a single mold.

---

[85] *Die Gottesfrage des heutigen Menschen* (Vienna: Herold, 1956). English translation: *Science, Religion and Christianity* (Westminster, Md.: Newman Press, 1958); and *The God Question and Modern Man* (New York: Seabury Press, 1967).

4. The Glory of the Lord

Why is the first part of this synthesis called *The Glory of the Lord* (*Herrlichkeit*)? Because it is concerned, first, with learning to see God's revelation and because God can be known only in his Lordliness and sublimity (*Herrheit* and *Hehr-heit*), in what Israel called *Kabod* and the New Testament *gloria*, something that can be recognized under all the incognitos of human nature and the Cross. This means that God does not come primarily as a teacher for us ("true"), as a useful "redeemer" for us ("good"), but to display and to radiate himself, the splendor of his eternal triune love in that "disinterestedness" that true love has in common with true beauty. For the glory of God the world was created; through it and for its sake the world is also redeemed. And only the person who is touched by a ray of this glory and has an incipient sensibility for what disinterested love is can learn to see the presence of divine love in Jesus Christ. *Aisthesis*, the act of perception, and *Aistheton*, the particular thing perceived (radiant love), together inform the object of theology. The "glorious" corresponds on the theological plane to what the transcendental "beautiful" is on the philosophical plane. But for the great thinkers of the West (from Homer and Plato via Augustine and Thomas down to Goethe and Hölderlin, Schelling and Heidegger), beauty is the last comprehensive attribute of all-embracing being as such, its last, mysterious radiance, which makes it loved as a whole despite the terrifying reality it may hide for the individual existent. Through the splendor of being, from within its primal depths, the strange signs of the biblical events (whose very contrariness to all human expectations, unique, incapable of either invention or dissolution by man, reveals their supraworldly origin) shine out with that glory of God whose praise and recognition fills the Scriptures, the Church's liturgy and the mottoes of the saintly founders of religious orders.

The first volume, *Schau der Gestalt* (*Seeing the Form*),[86] describes man's encounter with this most divine aspect of God. Starting with aesthetics may seem unusual or arbitrary; nonetheless, as is shown in *Glaubhaft ist nur Liebe* (*Love Alone*),[87] it is ultimately the only appropriate stance. Only such a stance can perceive the divine as such, without obscuring it beforehand by an instrumental relationship to the cosmos (which, imperfect, calls for divine completion) or to man (who, still more imperfect and lost in sin, requires a savior). The first desideratum for seeing objectively is the "letting be" of God's self-revelation, even if the latter is also "his eternal love for me". This first step is not to master the materials of perception by imposing our own categories on them but an attitude of service to the object. Theologically this means that the unspeakable mystery of God's love opens itself to reverence and adoration on the part of the subject (*timor filialis*). This means, too, that God's splendor (surpassing the transcendentality of "philosophical" beauty) reveals and authenticates itself definitively precisely in its own apparent antithesis (in the *kenosis* of the descent into hell) as love selflessly serving out of love. Thus *The Glory of the Lord* points not only to the proper center of theology but also to the heart of the individual's existential situation,

---

[86] *Herrlichkeit. Eine theologische Ästhetik*, vol. 1: *Schau der Gestalt* (Einsiedeln: Johannes Verlag, 1962; 3d ed., 1988). English translation: *The Glory of the Lord: A Theological Aesthetics*, vol. 1: *Seeing the Form* (San Francisco: Ignatius Press, New York: Crossroad Publications, 1982).

[87] See n. 15 above.

which we sought from the beginning and discussed in Section 1 of this retrospective. It can also be said that in *The Glory of the Lord* the Ignatian *ad majorem Dei gloriam* —as the last great motto of religious life since Benedict— is opened up to the Johannine interpretation of the total biblical unity *kabod-doxa-gloria* and thus to the final form of revelation's own self-interpretation.

The second volume, *Fächer der Stile* (*Studies in Theological Style*, volumes 2 and 3 of the English translation),[88] provides the evidence for the fact that truly epochal theology is illuminated by the glory of God, is touched in its depths by it and in a mysterious fashion takes something from it and gives it out again. But if a transcendental attribute of being cannot be defined in a categorical-conceptual way, how much less the *proprium* of the living God: the form and content of great theologies will always attest the one miracle in new and different ways and, even in eternity, will not together form a surveyable system. Thus the selection of the twelve representatives of Christian thought discussed in this volume has something arbitrary about it: together they form but a constellation. Irenaeus, Augustine, Dionysius, Anselm and Bonaventure are luminaries of the first magnitude (Origen had to be omitted, and I had already written fully on Maximus), but in the neo-scholasticism of the clerical figures after Thomas (who receives his due in volume 3/1

---

[88] *Herrlichkeit. Eine theologische Ästhetik*, vol. 2: *Fächer der Stile*, part 2: *Klerikale Stile* (Einsiedeln: Johannes Verlag, 1962; 3d ed., 1984) and part 2: *Laikale Stile* (Einsiedeln: Johannes Verlag, 1962; 3d ed., 1984). English translation: *The Glory of the Lord: A Theological Aesthetics*, vol. 2: *Studies in Theological Style: Clerical Styles* (San Francisco: Ignatius Press, New York: Crossroad, 1984); and vol. 3: *Studies in Theological Style: Lay Styles* (San Francisco: Ignatius Press, 1986).

[volume 4 of the English translation]), there is no longer such a direct radiance; hence laymen and religious come to the fore: Dante, John of the Cross, Pascal, Hamann and Soloviev (the watchmen at the dawn and dusk of German Idealism), Hopkins (who represents the mystical tradition of England and Ignatius himself) and Péguy (the representative of the contemporary Church in dialogue with the world). (Neither Möhler nor Scheeben would go far enough; Claudel glorifies the redeemed creation, not the form of salvation in a thematic sense; Chesterton does not produce a final form; but, as has been said, the choice here is not very important in itself.)

The emphasis in this volume is uniformly distributed. The reader will find that the unplatonic Irenaeus shines out especially brightly, that Dionysius appears indispensable to us because of his view of the Church as transparent to the sacred cosmos, that Anselm's prayerful thinking (now also in *Sigillum*) shines forth as a pure model, that Dante's daring act of taking before the throne of God the earthly love between man and woman and of purifying *Eros* so as to make of it something akin to *Agape* is a theological event of the first order, that John's annihilation of every created thing before the presence of God's glory is as necessary for us today as is Pascal's synthesis of mathematical and charismatic thinking, that Hamann is the only one of his century able to read the divine beauty out of its *kenosis*, that Soloviev knew how to embed the depths of German Idealism in the dimensions of his ecumenical thinking better than today's evolutionists. It would be much, indeed, if the nature of theological "style" were to be thought out anew: it is something quite different from the theological shop-talk and journalism of our time!

The third volume, *Im Raum der Metaphysik* (*The Realm*

of Metaphysics, volumes 4 and 5 of the English translation),[89] has a contrasting task: in the preceding volumes
the radiance of Christian thinking proceeded kerygmati-
cally from the (still invisible) sun of biblical revelation.
Now the Christian element must be immersed as deeply
as possible in the thinking of humanity. The splendor of
the divine in the world was (in Homer) the first formed
experience of the West; and it becomes evident that art is
begotten and itself begets only so long as it is created out
of a *mythos* lived and experienced. Philosophy (in the pre-
Socratics and, indeed, in a Plato still steeped in the light of
myth) replaces it, posing the ambiguous question of the
fundamental meaning of transcendence: man's power and
autonomy or God's revelation? Virgil and Plotinus pro-
vide the grand finale for antiquity with the same question.
What will Christianity do with the "*kalon*" of antiquity?
Forge from it a monstrance for the bread of "glory"?
Boethius, Erigena, the Victorines, Thomas, Nicholas of
Cusa: What precisely happens here? Is this *Eros* a raiment
of *Agape*? What place has the Cross? The catastrophe of
nominalism robs creation of every light of God; night
falls. Which ways remain? For the time being, three: the
Christian theology of self-abandonment (forming a single
spiritual family from Eckhart via the women mystics to
Ignatius and the *Grand Siècle*): But what is now the status
of the world? Secondly, the renewed anchoring of a now-

---

[89] *Herrlichkeit. Eine theologische Ästhetik*, vol. 3/1: *In Raum der Metaphysik*, part 1: *Alterium* (Einsiedeln: Johannes Verlag: 1965; 2d ed.,
1975) and part 2: *Neuzeit* (Einsiedeln: Johannes Verlag, 1965). English
translation: *The Glory of the Lord: A Theological Aesthetics*, vol. 4: *The
Realm of Metaphysics in Antiquity* (San Francisco: Ignatius Press, 1989),
and vol. 5: *The Realm of Metaphysics in the Modern Age* (San Francisco:
Ignatius Press, 1991).

unsupported theology in the foundations of antiquity (a strain that runs from Nicholas of Cusa through the Renaissance, the Baroque and the Enlightenment to Goethe and Heidegger): But then where is the distinctiveness of the Christian element? Finally, the philosophy of spirit (again from Eckhart and Nicholas of Cusa to Descartes, Leibniz, Spinoza and the Idealists): but if the (human) spirit masters all being conceptually, the splendor of Being is extinguished and is replaced by the "sublimity" of the thinker (Kant, Schiller), which with Hegel once again becomes entrapped in the past; what then remains is only grim materialistic fatality. The problem of the relation of metaphysics and theology allows no violent solution. And not because modern man thinks "thus" must the Christian proclamation, adapting itself, also think "thus". How can someone who is blind to Being be other than blind to God? Ought one not rather to say that the Christian, as proclaimer of God's glory today, in consequence takes upon himself—whether he wants to or not—the burden of metaphysics?

The final volume, *Theologie* (*Theology: The Old Covenant*, volume 6, and *Theology: The New Covenant*, volume 7 of the English translation),[90] is "dogmatic". It treats *gloria* first biblically, in the Old and New Testaments, culminating in the two final interpretations of what God's glory is; Paul (2 Corinthians 3) and John. Glory is eternal love descending into the uttermost darkness. The lit-

---

[90] *Herrlichkeit. Eine theologische Ästhetik*, vol. 3/2: *Theologie*, part 1: *Alter Bund* (Einsiedeln: Johannes Verlag, 1966, 2d ed., 1989); part 2: *Neuer Bund* (Einsiedeln: Johannes Verlag, 1969; 2d ed., 1983). English translation: *The Glory of the Lord: A Theological Aesthetics*, vol. 6: *Theology: The Old Covenant* (San Francisco: Ignatius Press, 1991); and vol. 7: *Theology: The New Covenant* (San Francisco: Ignatius Press, 1989).

urgy is a mirror for this. Then a quick passage through dogmatics. *Gloria* is (1) epiphany, nearness, being-with-us. Brotherly love is drawn into the eternal domain from which the light radiates. *Gloria* is (2) justification, incomprehensible *poiesis* of God. Here we need to engage in a dialogue with Luther: there is no other place than theological aesthetics where his ultimate meaning is seen in so positive a light; the "juridical" only obscures it. *Gloria* is (3) *charis*, with the entire double meaning of the ancient concept (Pindar) operative on a higher plane. Here it is necessary to enter into dialogue with the Eastern Church and her self-understanding, which is entirely determined by the concept of glory. Only in a supplementary way is the problem of Christian art to be treated: Is it possible and indeed, how is it possible for divine "splendor" to be expressed by means of worldly "beauty"?

The *Aesthetics* remains on the plane of light, image, vision. That is only *one* dimension of theology. The next involves deed, event, drama (Schelling says: positive philosophy). God acts for man; man responds through decision and deed. The history of the world and of man is itself a great "theater of the world"; here must be related to each other the philosophy of the deed (Fichte, Blondel), the art of the deed (Shakespeare, Calderon) and the theology of the deed (Karl Barth), to name just the catchwords. The Christian meaning of role and representation will have to be explained, and the Church's tradition must appear under this aspect: what an immense risk is the very act of handing on in death the task of discipleship to the next (faithful?) generation. Moses, Jesus and Paul experienced it most intensely. Is not the entire existence of the Church, as well as that of the individuals inside and outside her, pure deed and risk? And is not the same true of theology? Everything "good" stands and falls with freedom.

Only when these two parts have been finished can a *theological logic* be sketched. What, according to the Bible, is truth? What philosophical form does it have? For an approach, compare my book on the phenomenology of truth (*Wahrheit*),[91] whose first volume on the truth of the world points in turn to a second, unfinished volume on the truth of revelation. How does this philosophical form open itself to the incarnate form of Christ's truth? Then, too, how can human word and life witness credibly to this truth of God? Here again a vigorous discussion with Hegel and perhaps also with Origen would be required. But others will have to conduct it. In the short space that remains to a sixty-year-old, neither images nor concepts are any longer decisive; only the deed. For its sake, even the activity of writing books will have to be buried: God grant that then not only paper rot but that at least one grain of wheat achieve the grace of the Resurrection! All paper belongs to the broad way. It is not important that the patient record of our thought be printed [*bedruckt*] but rather that the impatient flesh be squeezed and compressed [*bedrückt und gepresst*] so that from it perhaps a few fruitful drops might flow forth. Compressed it must be, in order not to miss the narrow way, the strait gate, perhaps even the microscopic needle's eye that, invisible to the eye of men, leads into the Kingdom.

[91] *Wahrheit. Erstes Buch: Wahrheit der welt* (Einsiedeln: Benziger, 1947; 2d ed., Einsiedeln: Johannes Verlag, 1985) (= *Theologik*, vol. 1: *Wahrheit der Welt*).

5. A Word of Thanks

All charisms of Christians are inextricably interwoven; everyone owes himself not only to God but to the whole Church; everyone is borne by invisible prayers and sacrifices, has been nourished by countless gifts of love, is continually strengthened and preserved by the affection of others. "All men are cannibals" (Baader). Who is able to say thanks? To repay the immeasurable realm of deceased and surviving individuals with the homage they deserve for the graces they have mediated? Where is the wonderful being known as Homer, that he might be thanked; where the chaste Virgil and the God-filled heart of Plotinus? Love and honor must suffice for them.

And where would a man end, if he wanted to begin thanking those of his fellow men who accompanied him on his way, formed him, protected him, made everything possible? Left and right the greetings would have to go: to the nameable and the nameless. A mother is there, who during the course of a long fatal illness dragged herself to Church each morning to pray for her children. Other close relatives, of whom (to what ends God knows) fearful sufferings were demanded. Only in the light of God will one really know what he has to be thankful for.

A few names must be acknowledged, however, because without them obviously nothing of what has been sketched out here would have been possible. To the student in Vienna, the friendship with Rudolf Allers, doctor, psychiatrist, philosopher and theologian (he translated Thomas and the entire corpus of Anselm's works) was an almost inexhaustible source of stimulation. An opponent of Freud and a free disciple of Alfred Adler, he possessed and imparted the feeling for interhuman love as the objective medium of human existence; it was in this turning from the "I" to the reality full of a "thou" that he saw philosophical truth and psychotherapeutic method. Later, in Munich, Peter Lippert became a consoler of the young man languishing in the desert of neo-scholasticism, and Erich Przywara an unforgettable guide and master. Never since have I encountered such a combination of depth and fullness of analytic clarity and all-embracing synoptic vision. My publication of three volumes of his works is intended as an external sign of thanks; but none of my own books should hide what it owes to him. In Lyons during my theological studies, it was the encounter with Henri de Lubac that decided the direction of my studies. Because exegesis was weak, the Fathers easily won the upper hand. Origen (who was for me, as once for Erasmus, more important than Augustine) became the key to the entire Greek patristics, the early Middle Ages and, indeed, even to Hegel and Karl Barth.

In Basel, the mission of Adrienne von Speyr (which, in view of her books, can no longer remain incomprehensible to a Christian public) was decisive. What Ignatius had intended in his time meant henceforth for me "secular institute"; the hard sacrifice demanded by this transition was accompanied by the certainty of serving the same idea more exactly. It was Adrienne von Speyr who showed the way in which Ignatius is fulfilled by John and therewith laid the basis for most of what I have published since 1940. Her work and mine are neither psychologically nor philologically to be separated: two halves of a single whole, which has as its center a unique foundation.

It is almost unnecessary to set out how much I owe to Karl Barth: as I have already said, the vision of a comprehensive biblical theology, combined with the urgent invitation to engage in a dogmatically serious ecumenical dialogue, without which the entire movement would lack foundation. He joyfully greeted and endorsed my book about him, followed my subsequent works with some suspicion but perhaps never noticed how much a little book like *Glaubhaft ist nur Liebe (Love Alone)*[92] sought to be fair to him and represents perhaps the closest approach to his position from the Catholic side.

Albert Béguin, whom I had the joy of baptizing, the great solitary whose heart beat in unison with all who suffered injustice in the world, with every humiliated and insulted individual, the one who in the years of distress united the spiritual forces of the resistance in his *Cahiers du Rhône*, who as soon as the borders were opened immediately travelled to Auschwitz *"pour nous bien placer dans l'axe de détresse"* (Péguy),[93] who then as Mounier's successor took over *Esprit*: this man was to me an example of what the spiritual courage of a Christian is—something that can rest on nothing other than the absoluteness of his mission. Péguy, Bernanos, Bloy were his kindred spirits; he made them accessible to many, including myself, and, indeed, made them indispensable to me beyond every fashion of the day.

The many friends whose names I now omit will certainly not fault me if I mention only one more name: Gustav Siewerth, the man with the brain of a lion and the heart of a child, fearful in his philosophical anger against those who had forgotten Being and, thereby, the freer to speak happily and tenderly of the innermost mystery of

[92] See n. 15 above.
[93] Charles Péguy. "Les Cinq prières dans la Cathédrale de Chartres". III: "Prière de confidence", in: *Oeuvres poétiques complètes*, Pléiade (Paris: Gallimard, 1941), 698.

reality: of the God of love, of the heart as the center of man, of the pain of existence, of the Cross borne by the Father's child. Without him the third volume of *Herrlichkeit* (volumes 4 and 5 of *The Glory of the Lord*) would not have received this present form.

But now it is time to say what is my final word of thanks here, to Berthe Widmer, who has taken on herself the thankless toil of gathering even the smallest of my *disjecta membra* or (as Père Congar would say) my *ossa humiliata* and of displaying them cleanly in the "first ossuary" that now opens its doors to the reader.

IV

ANOTHER TEN YEARS

1975

As everybody knows, at the age of seventy a man has attained, according to the Bible, the apex of his life, so this should also be the right point, the final point, at which once more to draw up a balance-sheet. Personally, I thought I had presented this retrospective review to my contemporaries ten years ago—since for oneself there must be self-questioning every day—and owed nothing more of substance, from this point of view, to the world at large. At that time I published *In Retrospect* (Chapter 3, above), which recounts the fundamental motives for the great decisions of my life (that, by the grace of God, can be considered definitive), the most fruitful encounters with contemporary personalities, the choice of literary themes insofar as such a choice has been free and not conditioned, as is often the case in small works, by external stimuli. These exterior stimuli, with the passing of the years, have become ever more numerous, so that the literary legacy of the last ten years derives almost exclusively from responses to a wide variety of requests and petitions—so much so that I have just been left with

Translated by John Saward; published in English in *The Analogy of Beauty: The Theology of Hans Urs von Balthasar*, edited by John Riches (Edinburgh: T. & T. Clark, 1986). This article has been revised by Fr. Brian McNeil, C.R.V., to conform to the German edition of *Mein Werk*.

finding free moments for developing what was considered the fundamental project, the goal of my life, what I
had declared, a little presumptuously and rashly, to be the
plan of a theological trilogy, on the outcome of which I
will speak later.

Before doing so, I would like to mention two other
points. First, one is so taken with a fixed idea that it is
present (as in the *Symphonie fantastique* of Berlioz) even in
works that are not so-called masterpieces. This idea also
permeates secondary works—to their advantage or dis-
advantage—and becomes a kind of signature, a style that
keeps the most disparate themes united. From this, one
can also deduce whether this formative idea is at a suffi-
ciently "catholic" distance to embrace questions that are
very remote from one another, apparently contradictory.
At this point the connection between style and truth becomes visible, and the writer must submit himself to the
judgment of his own ideas. In this judgment one will also
have to decide whether this idea is "actual" in a more profound sense, that it is not the fashion of the day. Themes
can encounter history and then in some way run parallel
to it. By ignoring his historical present, a writer might
in fact pursue such a theme and claim it as one of his
"timeless certainties".

But one must also be on the look-out for the other
eventuality, where this fundamental theme, which ini-
tially did not seem particularly "actual", reveals itself in
the course of the years to be more and more actual in
the historical sense and in this way receives a definite
kind of confirmation, even though it is not of course
the ultimate confirmation that will be given by the judgment of God. However, a judgment of this kind cannot come from the writer himself (anyone, in fact, who

wants to have an influence on his time considers himself actual); no, it comes from his contemporaries or from posterity. Such a judgment, if it is worth the trouble, ought to refer to *A Short Guide to My Books* (Chapter 2, above), published twenty years ago, for once something has been offered to the public, one has neither the right nor the possibility of taking it away from their attention.

The second premise is the simple repetition of the confession made ten years ago: the activity of being a writer remains and will always remain, in the working-out of my life, a secondary function, something *faute de mieux*. At its center there is a completely different interest: the task of renewing the Church through the formation of new communities that unite the radical Christian life of conformity to the evangelical counsels of Jesus with existence in the midst of the world, whether by practicing secular professions or through the ministerial priesthood to give new life to living communities. All my activity as a writer is subordinated to this task; if authorship had to give way before the urgency of the task of which I have spoken, to me it would not seem as if anything had been lost; no, much would have been gained. This is fundamentally obvious to one who lives in service of the cause of Jesus, the cause that concretely is the Church.

However, granted that here one can and must speak solely of the writer and not of his work in the Church, this can be done from the two following points of view: from the point of view, first, of the fundamental disposition described farther on and, then, from the point of view of the spreading out of that disposition and style of thinking in the multiplicity of responses to the demands of the present.

1. In the meanwhile, *Herrlichkeit: Eine theologische Ästhetik*[1] has been completed (the advertised concluding volume on ecumenism will very probably not be published). In the preface to the first volume it was expressly introduced as the first panel of a triptych, and only as such is it justified in the economy of a Christian theology. And so to call the *Theological Aesthetics* the masterpiece, the work of my life (very often only the introductory volume has been read, and on the basis of that all the rest is presupposed), for which the author is famed as a "theological aesthete", to do this is to misunderstand my fundamental intention. It is difficult to see how such a definition could occur to anyone who has read at least the two concluding parts on the Old and New Covenants. What is involved is primarily not "beauty" in the modern or even in the philosophical (transcendental) sense but the surpassing of beauty in "glory" in the sense of the splendor of the divinity of God himself as manifested in the life, death, and Resurrection of Jesus

---

[1] *Herrlichkeit. Eine theologische Ästhetik* (Einsiedeln, Johannes Verlag) vol. 1: *Schau der Gestalt* (1961; 3d ed., 1988); vol. 2: *Fächer der Stile*; part 1: *Klerikale Stile* (1962; 3d ed., 1984); part 2: *Laikale Stile* (1962; 3d ed., 1984); vol. 3/1: *Im Raum der Metaphysik*; part 1: *Altertum* (1965; 2d ed., 1975); part 2: *Neuzeit* (1965; 2d ed., 1975); vol. 3/2: *Theologie*; part 1: *Alter Bund* (1966; 2d ed., 1989); part 2: *Neuer Bund* (1969; 2d ed., 1988).

English translation: *The Glory of the Lord: A Theological Aesthetics* (vols. 1–2: San Francisco: Ignatius Press, New York: Crossroad; vols. 3–7: San Francisco, Ignatius Press). Vol. 1: *Seeing the Form* (1982); vol. 2: *Studies in Theological Style: Clerical Styles* (1984); vol. 3: *Studies in Theological Style: Lay Styles* (1986); vol. 4: *The Realm of Metaphysics in Antiquity* (1989); vol. 5: *The Realm of Metaphysics in the Modern Age* (1991); vol. 6: *Theology: The Old Covenant* (1991); vol. 7: *Theology: The New Covenant* (1989).

and reflected, according to Paul, in Christians who look upon their Lord.

But the manifestation of God, theophany, is only the prelude to the central event: the encounter, in creation and in history, between infinite divine freedom and finite human freedom. This central issue is dealt with in *Theodramatik* (*Theo-Drama*),[2] the first volume of which, *Prolegomena*, was published in 1973. God does not want to be just "contemplated" and "perceived" by us, like a solitary actor by his public; no, from the beginning he has provided for a play in which we must all share. This has already been clearly demonstrated in the *Aesthetics*, above all in the concluding volumes, which focus on the Bible. But such a play must now be dealt with directly, thematically, especially since the lack in our time of an explicit "theo-dramatics" appears more and more glaring and painful, with the principal tendencies in modern theology—all more or less detached from the "epic" of scholastic thought—seeming to converge on such a dramatics, yet without attaining it. In the introduction to the first volume, the following tendencies were enumerated: the theology of event, historicism, orthopraxy, the concern with dialogue, the theology of hope and of the future, functionalism (structuralism), the sociology and psychology of roles, the preoccupation with the problems

[2] *Theodramatik* (Einsiedeln, Johannes Verlag) vol. 1: *Prolegomena* (1973); vol. 2: *Die Personen des Spiels*; part 1: *Der Mensch in Gott* (1976); part 2: *Die Personen in Christus* (1978); vol. 3: *Die Handlung* (1980); vol. 4: *Das Endspiel* (1983).

English translation: *Theo-Drama: Theological Dramatic Theory* (San Francisco, Ignatius Press). Vol. 1: *Prolegomena* (1988); vol. 2: *Dramatis Personae: Man in God* (1990); vol. 3: *Dramatis Personae: Persons in Christ* (1992); vol. 4: *The Action* (1993); vol. 5: *The Last Act* (in preparation).

of freedom and of evil in the world. All these tendencies are aiming, like arrows, for a central point at which a theological dramatics, which has not yet been elaborated, ought to be found; only there can the individual tendencies meet, integrate and be fruitful.

It seems to me that, instead of suddenly rushing into the construction of such a theology, one should first elaborate a "dramatic instrumentation" of the literary and lived theater, and thus of life itself, in order to prepare images and concepts with which one can then work (with an adequate transposition). This would be an occasion, with many possibilities, for speaking, among other things, of drama as the clarification of existence, of that strange trio —the author, the actor, the producer—and also of public performance and the horizon of comprehension. Then there is the question of the purpose of the dramatic action —of situation, freedom, destiny, death, the struggle for "good" and for "right" fought out in the dramatic action, of tragedy, comedy, tragicomedy. But the best approach to Christian theology is in terms of the problematic of roles, so widely discussed today: Who am I? (someone, a *unicum*, or, in the final analysis, no one?). What is the task that justifies, fulfills, forms my existence? And this question applies at both the individual and social levels.

Only when God appears on the world stage (and at the same time remains behind the scenes) can one work out what *the persons of the drama* stand for, what "laws" this dramatic action follows, a dramatic action ultimately without parallel, because it constitutes the ultimate drama. All this is what every Christian knows in a spontaneous and unselfconscious way and what he strives to live out. What I am trying to do is to express this in a form in which all the dimensions and tensions of life remain present instead of being sublimated in the abstractions of a "systematic" theology.

If such an enterprise is to be brought to completion, despite age, there must follow, as a third and final part, "Theo-logy",[3] at which so many people nowadays labor intensely. This "Theo-logy" involves reflection on the way in which the dramatic event can be transposed into human words and concepts for the purposes of comprehension, proclamation and contemplation. It should therefore be a methodical, a posteriori reflection on what has been done in the first and second parts. This can happen because God has essentially and definitively pronounced his Word in time, and "Theo-logy" certainly has something to do with the Logos.

In the course of expounding the dramatic Christian event, one is bound to confront already existing forms of thought and theological exposition, the modern attempts already mentioned, but also, and above all, the great contemporary non-Christian attempts at a synthetic interpretation of existence. The most important of these are oriental (pagan) religiosity (with its primarily contemplative constitution) and the (Judaic) Marxism that has arisen in the West (with its tendency toward activity and innovation). These two interpretations, with every possible seduction, woo the Christian soul tired of its Christian inheritance.

There is much talk of the "de-Mediterraneanization" of the Church. I can only believe in this conditionally. Let us not forget that Palestine, too (with its relations with the East), is on the Mediterranean, and it was in

---

[3] *Theologik* (Einsiedeln, Johannes Verlag) vol. 1: *Wahrheit der Welt* (1985); vol. 2: *Wahrheit Gottes* (1985); vol. 3: *Der Geist der Wahrheit* (1987). English translation in preparation.

Palestine that very diverse passages of the writings of the New Testament were formed. But the Christian proclamation can never be de-biblicized; in other words, you can never take away its dramatic character, representing, as it does, the struggle between heaven and earth, a struggle that goes on, moreover, in the personal dimension as well as in the social. And so the personal is brought back to itself by the social and vice versa, the contemplative by the active and vice versa, so that the Christian dramatic shows itself to be, as it were, by its very nature, at the center between, and raised above, the two fundamental attempts to give meaning to the world and to existence, attempts that are possible when you start with the world itself.

2. And so we reach the second aspect: the breaking up of the fundamental purpose into the multiplicity of what is "actual". Reviews and journals, for the most part, ask the theologian for contributions and standpoints on burning questions of the day. In such an undertaking I am very far from the creative imagination and power of composition of a Karl Rahner and only dare to move gropingly in such a field. Nonetheless, the last decade has reinforced this fundamental conviction of mine: You do good apologetics if you do good, central theology; if you expound theology effectively, you have done the best kind of apologetics. The Word of God (which is also and always the activity of God) is self-authenticating proof of its own truth and fecundity—and it is precisely in this way that the Church and the believer are inserted into one another. The man who wants this Word to be heard in what he has to say, starting with himself, does not need to resort to another discipline (called Fundamental Theology) to gain a hearing for it. All the other

promises prove to be insufficient in themselves and give
way before the Word of God by the very fact that this
Word presents itself to men and to humanity together
with its promises. Only the Word of God makes a personal impact on man of such force that he feels himself
touched by it in the center of his heart, and it is just no
longer enough for him to sink into an impersonal identity in the manner of the Far East or to wear himself out
through a transformation of humanity (for him as a person, unattainable) in the manner of the Marxist West.
What these two human contributions, which confront
one another as opposite poles, can never attain is offered
only "by the final stone sent from the vault of heaven on
high" (Claudel), namely, by the Word of the Father, who
became man to bring to completion, together with his
Church, the ever perfectible edifice of the world and of
history. And the Church has always remained that unity
which to Jews and pagans seemed impossible.

In the last few years this theme has frequently been
expounded in a variety of forms, for example in "Three
Forms of Hope" (in *Die Wahrheit ist symphonisch* [*Truth
Is Symphonic*]),[4] more extensively in "The Claim to
Catholicity" (in *Pneuma und Institution* [*Pneuma and institution*]),[5] finally, in rapid and almost sloganistic fashion, in
my last little book, *Katholisch* (*In the Fullness of Faith: On
the Centrality of the Distinctively Catholic*).[6] And so an an-

---

[4] *Die Wahrheit ist symphonisch. Aspekte des christlichen Pluralismus.* Kriterien 29 (Einsiedeln: Johannes Verlag, 1972), 147–65. English translation: *Truth Is Symphonic: Aspects of Christian Pluralism* (San Francisco:
Ignatius Press, 1987).

[5] *Pneuma und Institution.* Skizzen zur Theologie 4 (Einsiedeln: Johannes Verlag, 1974). English translation in preparation.

[6] *Katholisch. Aspekte des Mysteriums.* Kriterien 36 (Einsiedeln: Jo-

cient, almost atrophied principle of apologetics has been revitalized: it is right to see beyond positions that elsewhere seem isolated, absolutized. The notorious Catholic "And"—in contrast to all unilateral, heretical positions —is not in fact a lukewarm compromise or syncretism but rather the power to unite, once again in "dramatic" fashion, what to men seems desperately fragmentary. Jesus Christ is, in this sense, the Catholic One: God and man, he who descended into hell and ascended into heaven, he himself explores the personal and social dimensions of human existence and reestablishes them out of his own experience.

Of course, there is no question here of a Catholic presumption, in the face of all the other Christian and non-Christian and non-Christian positions, trying to deliver itself from them by calling them partial. For the position of God and Jesus Christ can never be the position of an individual Christian, and non-Catholic positions serve, nearly always, to remind the Catholic (often very drastically) of all that he has lost sight of, whether culpably or by forgetfulness; they remind him how far he is still from his own center.

Authentic catholicity is so urgent for the Catholic that he must acquire it before he can afford to engage in dialogue with other confessions or visions of the world. Otherwise he runs the risk of his Catholicism being considered as one "confession" among others and then of attempting, together with these other confessions, a higher synthesis—this is the delusion with which "ecumenical

hannes Verlag, 1975). English translation: *In the Fullness of Faith: On the Centrality of the Distinctively Catholic* (San Francisco: Ignatius Press, 1988).

dialogue" is often encumbered today. Precisely because this dialogue is nowadays not only important but indispensable, the Catholic must first of all be prepared for it. He cannot enter and take part in it with a purely empirical and theologically dilettante awareness of what catholicity and the Catholic Church in general are.

My efforts in these last few years have been deliberately concerned with this premise for ecumenical dialogue and for the dialogues with all the non-Christian visions of the world. In this context my efforts are chiefly a discourse *ad intra*, within the Church. We need above all to arouse a new sensitivity to the multiplicity and polyphony of divine truth, in conscious opposition to the vociferous stance taken up about ecclesiastical and ecumenical "pluralism". One can formulate the following obvious, basic affirmation: the more an organism becomes differentiated and alive in its individual organs and functions, the more it must possess a more profound internal unity. Individual aspects of this basic affirmation have been developed in the collection *Die Wahrheit ist symphonisch* (*Truth Is Symphonic*);[7] in the second part of this book, particularly striking and relevant examples are expounded. This problem becomes especially intense when confronted with the dichotomy that threatens all of modern cultural life (with its technicalization, cybernetics, and so on), the dichotomy that in the Christian/ecclesiastical consciousness is translated into the dualism of "pneuma" and "institution". Precisely what in Christ and in the Church, the living organism in which a spiritual soul manifests itself (and *must* manifest itself corporeally in order to be itself), is and must remain united at all costs is wrenched

[7] See n. 4 above.

apart. The spiritual movements that are so numerous today (whether they be orientated toward the East or toward the Pentecost event) very often (though not always)
take up a defensive position, voluntary or involuntary,
in confrontation with a Church seen and understood as
institution—and obviously the postconciliar troubles inside the Church serve to reinforce this misunderstanding in a decisive way. In *Spiritus Creator*,[8] more directly
in *Pneuma und Institution*[9] and *Der antirömische Affekt* (*The
Office of Peter and the Structure of the Church*),[10] I tried to re-
sist this disastrous resentment, which misrepresents the
living, organic "form" by equating it with a structure
constructed with reason alone. In *Der antirömische Affekt*
it was not at all a question of a pure defense of the isolated principle of the papacy, as if this were an individual
element that could be added in its own right to the rest
or from which one could abstract. It was instead a question of demonstrating in general terms the organic unity
of the revelation of God in Jesus Christ, of investigat-
ing the different aspects and stratifications of this unity,
and only after that of integrating the Petrine factor of
unity with the other wider factors. Back in 1969, my
little book, *Einfaltungen* (*Convergences*),[11] had pushed in a
similar direction; in it I wanted to show that there can be

---

[8] *Spiritus Creator*. Skizzen zur Theologie 3 (Einsiedeln: Johannes Verlag, 1967). English translation: *Creator Spirit*. Explorations in Theology
3 (San Francisco: Ignatius Press, 1993).

[9] See n. 5 above.

[10] *Der antirömische Affekt. Wie lässt sich das Papsttum in der Gesamtkirche
integrieren?* (Freiburg: Herder-Bücherei [vol. 492], 1974); 2, enlarged
ed. (Einsiedeln: Johannes Verlag, 1989). English translation: *The Office
of Peter and the Structure of the Church* (San Francisco: Ignatius Press,
1986).

[11] *Einfaltungen. Auf Wegen christlicher Einigung* (Munich: Kösel-Verlag,

no theology without spirituality, that the multiplicity of theological disciplines can exist only thanks to the unity of theological science, that the numerous biblical theologies are only partial aspects of a unity of divine truth existing in the Spirit in the Church but never systematizable. They are then brought into conscious convergence by the fact that the multiplicity of dogmas is only the mediation of the unique "dogma", Jesus Christ, by all the parts. It is clear that the Christian art of integration (into catholicity) is something completely different from what people nowadays like to call "integralism". Integralism is the debilitating, mechanical attempt to hold together a disparate collection of individual truths and traditions; integration, in contrast, is the spontaneous art of aiming always at the Whole through the fragments of truth discussed and lived. The Whole, then, is always greater than us and our powers of expression, but precisely as it greater animates our Christian life.

3. A concluding word is necessary in order to remove the impression that in the books that I have mentioned, and in others, I have simply expounded my own convictions. The greater part of so much of what I have written is a translation of what is present in more immediate, less technical fashion in the powerful work of Adrienne von Speyr, only part of which has been published. In the last ten years work on the patrimony bequeathed by this exceptional woman has been almost completed. Frau Barbara Albrecht has taken on the task of extracting from the complete works an anthology of representative texts and of writing a volume of commentary for

1969; 4th ed., Einsiedeln: Johannes Verlag, 1988). English translation: *Convergences* (San Francisco: Ignatius Press, 1983).

it.[12] Jaca Books of Milan has had the courage to publish this selection of texts in Italian[13] with an introduction by me.[14] French[15] and American[16] editions of the same anthology are also in preparation (the Germans have little interest in the work, the Swiss none at all). The richness contained there will only be recognized in more mature times. Then it will be seen how strongly the intuition of this woman has influenced my books—*Herz der Welt* (*Heart of the World*),[17] *Gottesfrage* (*The God Question*),[18] *Theologie der drei Tage* (*Mysterium Paschale*)[19]—and various other works, which essentially are only a theological transcription of so much learned directly from her.

[12] Barbara Albrecht, *Eine Theologie des Katholischen. Einführung in das Werk Adrienne von Speyrs* (Einsiedeln: Johannes Verlag); vol. 1: *Durchblick in Texten* (1972); vol. 2: *Darstellung* (1973).

[13] Adrienne von Speyr, *Mistica oggettiva* (Milan: Jaca Book, 1975; 2d ed. 1989). The biographical part from *Erster Blick auf Adrienne von Speyr* with a selection of text from Barbara Albrecht (cf. n. 12, above).

[14] *Erster Blick auf Adrienne von Speyr* (Einsiedeln: Johannes Verlag, 1968; 4th ed., 1989). English translation: *First Glance at Adrienne von Speyr* (San Francisco: Ignatius Press, 1981).

[15] Hans Urs von Balthasar, *Adrienne von Speyr et sa mission théologique.* (Paris: Apostolat des Editions / Montreal: Editions Paulines, 1976; 3d ed., Médiaspaul, 1985). The biographical part of *Erster Blick auf Adrienne von Speyr* with a selection of text by Barbara Albrecht (cf. n. 12, above).

[16] *First Glance at Adrienne von Speyr.*

[17] *Das Herz der Welt* (Zurich: Arche Verlag, 1945), 4th ed., with new foreword (Ostfildern: Schwabenverlag, 1988). English translation: *Heart of the World* (San Francisco: Ignatius Press, 1979).

[18] *Die Gottesfrage des heutigen Menschen* (Vienna: Herold, 1956). English translation: *Science, Religion and Christianity* (Westminster, Md.: Newman Press, 1958); and *The God Question and Modern Man* (New York: Seabury Press, 1967).

[19] *Theologie der drei Tage.* In: *Mysterium Salutis* 3 (Einsiedeln: Benziger, 1969; new ed., Freiburg: Johannes Verlag Einsiedeln, 1990).

This is an assertion that can only be verified at a later date.

On the other hand, what can be proved here and now is that the works of both of us are fundamentally opposed to the separation, common nowadays but lethal for the *Catholica*, of spirit and institution. While Adrienne von Speyr demonstrates the inseparability of the two aspects, beginning above all with John, to the same end I have made use chiefly of the Pauline epistles (2 Corinthians), the ecclesiological relevance of which is conspicuous enough. Wherever the convergence of the two aspects is visible—for example, in the Communione e Liberazione movement (to which in 1971 I dedicated my programmatic book *In Gottes Einsatz leben* [*Engagement with God*][20]), —there is hope for the comprehension of catholicity. The Incarnation of the Logos, his nuptial relation with the Church (and through the Church with the world), involves the organic character of the Church. The more the Church has to keep herself Catholic, open to all, dialogical, dramatic, in the modern world, the more profoundly she must comprehend and live her intimate essence as Body and Bride of Christ.

Having said that, we can go a stage farther. The works of Adrienne von Speyr, almost all of which were dictated to me, represent about a third of the books written with my own hand; a second, weak third is made up of the books published under my own name; a more full-bodied third, finally, is made up of books translated by me for my publishing house. And if now I search my heart, there are in this last category many books that are dearer and

[20] *In Gottes Einsatz leben*, Kriterien 24 (Einsiedeln: Johannes Verlag, 1971; 2d ed., 1972). English translation: *Engagement with God* (London: S.P.C.K., 1975).

more important to me than my own books. There are
the works of my friends, such as Henri de Lubac and
Louis Bouyer, of the great poets, such as Claudel, Péguy,
Bernanos, without speaking of Maurice Blondel or of
Ignatius, Calderon and John of the Cross, to whom also
I have dared to draw near. Then again there are works of
less well-known authors whose voices, so it seems to me,
ought not to be missing from the contemporary concert.
For a great number of authors whom I have edited, I
have each time written a preface in order to situate them
more correctly, with their specific tonality, in the orches·
tra. In this way, my publishing, which takes up much of
my time, is more important to me than the completion
of my own works. It offers a condensation of what I understand by contemporary Catholic spirituality (in theology, philosophy and literature). In a concert one instrument must no longer sound like just *one* instrument—
the ensemble is involved, the whole orchestra. Were I to
be asked which volumes of the *Ästhetik* (*The Glory of the
Lord*), I love most, I would reply: the one (volumes 2
and 3 of the English translation) in which I tried to expound twelve great theologians, beginning with Irenaeus
and ending with Soloviev; in their integrity they let the
sound of what I have wanted to make heard ring out.
Were I to be asked which of my own books gives me
greatest joy, which I still take up from time to time, the
answer would be: without doubt my Origen anthology,
Origenes, Geist und Feuer (*Origen: Spirit and Fire*),[21] for in

[21] *Origenes, Geist und Feuer. Ein Aufbau aus seinen Werken* (Salzburg:
Otto Müller, 1938; revised and expanded ed., 1953). English translation: *Origen: Spirit and Fire: A Thematic Anthology of His Writings* (Washington, D.C.: Catholic University of America Press, 1984). Cf. also:
Parole et mystère chez Origène (Paris: Éditions du Cerf, 1957).

Origen I discovered that brilliant sense of what is Catholic, which I myself would like to attain; but also my translations of the poems of Claudel—among which, it seems to me, there are some of incomparable beauty—which breathe the same spirit of catholicity. Both these authors lived the Church above all as a *communio sanctorum*.

And since we have met with that word "communion", we must, finally, mention our review *Communio*, of which I am a "co-founder", together with other members of the International Theological Commission, and which almost every year comes out in a new language. It is not a question of a uniform review, mechanically translated into several languages, but of a living association of reviews that choose and discuss their themes in the same spirit of catholicity; according to need, they exchange articles and so realize, across nations, cultures and continents, what I have tried to do at a more restricted level. Those who collaborate on the review in the spirit of a living Church are all much younger than I, so there is hope: when before long the old trunk, by now sterile, is chopped down, a living tree will be able to continue to grow unharmed; it may even, perhaps, spread out its branches more quickly.

V

RETROSPECTIVE

1988

When a man has published many large books, people will ask themselves: What, fundamentally, did he want to say? If he is a prolific novelist—for example, Dickens or Dostoyevsky—one would choose one or another of his works without worrying oneself too much about all of them as a whole. But for a philosopher or theologian it is totally different. One wishes to touch the heart of his thought, because one presupposes that such a heart must exist.

The question has often been asked of me by those disconcerted by the large number of my books: Where must one start in order to understand you? I am going to attempt to condense my many fragments "in a nutshell", as the English say, as far as that can be done without too many betrayals. The danger of such a compression consists in being too abstract. It is necessary to amplify what follows with my biographical works, on the one hand (on the Fathers of the Church, on Karl Barth, Buber, Bernanos, Guardini, Reinhold Schneider, and all the authors treated in the trilogy), with the works on spirituality, on the other hand (such as those on contempla-

Translated by Kelly Hamilton; first published in English in *Communio* 15 (Winter 1988): 468–73. Copyright 1988 by Communio: International Catholic Review. This last essay was presented on May 10, 1988, in Madrid on the occasion of the opening of a symposium on Hans Urs von Balthasar's theology—ED.

tive prayer, on Christ, Mary and the Church), and finally, with the numerous translations of the Fathers of
the Church, of the theologians of the Middle Ages and
of modern times. But here it is necessary to limit our-
selves to presenting a schema of the trilogy: Aesthetic,
Dramatic, and Logic.

We start with a reflection on the situation of man. He
exists as a limited being in a limited world, but his reason is open to the unlimited, to all of Being. The proof
consists in the recognition of his finitude, of his contin-
gence: I am, but I could also, however, not be. Many
things that do not exist could exist. Essences are limited,
but Being is not. That division, the "real distinction" of
St. Thomas, is the source of all the religious and philosophical thought of humanity. It is not necessary to recall
that all human philosophy (if we abstract the biblical domain and its influence) is essentially at once religious and
theological, because it poses the problem of the Absolute
Being, whether one attributes to it a personal character
or not.

What are the major solutions to this enigma attempted
by humanity? One can try to leave behind the division
between Being and essence, between the infinite and the
finite; one will then say that all Being is infinite and im-
mutable (Parmenides) or that all is movement, rhythm
between contraries, becoming (Heraclitus).

In the first case, the finite and limited will be non-
being as such, thus an illusion that one must detect: this
is the solution of Buddhist mysticism with its thousand
nuances in the Far East. It is also the Plotinian solution:
the truth is only attained in ecstasy where one touches
the One, which is at the same time All and Nothing (relative to all the rest that only seems to exist). The second

case contradicts itself: pure becoming in pure finitude can only conceive of itself in identifying the contraries: life and death, good fortune and adversity, wisdom and folly (Heraclitus did this).

Thus it is necessary to commence from an inescapable duality: the finite is not the infinite. In Plato, the sensible, terrestrial world is not the ideal, divine world. The question is then inevitable: Whence comes the division? Why are we not God?

The first attempt at a response: There must have been a fall, a decline, and the road to salvation can only be the return of the sensible finite into the intelligible infinite. That is the way of all nonbiblical mystics. The second attempt at a response: The infinite God had need of a finite world. Why? To perfect himself, to actualize all of his possibilities? Or even to have an object to love? The two solutions lead to pantheism. In both cases, the Absolute, God in himself, has again become indigent, thus finite. But if God has no need of the world—yet again: Why does the world exist?

No philosophy could give a satisfactory response to that question. St. Paul would say to the philosophers that God created man so that he would *seek* the Divine, try to attain the Divine. That is why all pre-Christian philosophy is theological at its summit. But, in fact, the true response to philosophy could only be given by Being himself, revealing himself from himself. Will man be capable of understanding this revelation? The affirmative response will be given only by the God of the Bible. On the one hand, this God, Creator of the world and of man, knows his creature. "I who have created the eye, do I not see? I who have created the ear, do I not hear?" And we add "I who have created language, could I not speak and make myself heard?" And this posits a counterpart: To be able to hear and understand the auto-revelation of God, man must in himself be a search for God, a question posed to him. Thus there is no biblical theology without a religious philosophy. Human reason must be open to the infinite.

It is here that the substance of my thought inserts itself. Let us say above all that the traditional term "metaphysical" signified the act of transcending physics, which for the Greeks signified the totality of the cosmos, of which man was a part. For us, physics is something else: the science of the material world. For us, the cosmos perfects itself in man, who at the same time sums up the world and surpasses it. Thus our philosophy will be essentially a meta-anthropology, presupposing not only the cosmological sciences but also the anthropological sciences, and surpassing them toward the question of the being and essence of man.

Now man exists only in dialogue with his neighbor. The infant is brought to consciousness of himself only by love, by the smile of his mother. In that encounter, the horizon of all unlimited being opens itself for him, revealing four things to him: (1) that he is one in love with the mother, even in being other than his mother, therefore all being is one; (2) that that love is good, therefore all Being is good; (3) that that love is true, therefore all Being is true; and (4) that that love evokes joy, therefore all Being is beautiful.

We add here that the epiphany of Being has sense only if in the appearance [*Erscheinung*] we grasp the essence that manifests itself [*Ding an sich*]. The infant comes to the knowledge, not of a pure appearance, but of his mother in herself. That does not exclude our grasping the essence only through the manifestation and not in itself (St. Thomas).

The One, the Good, the True and the Beautiful, these are what we call the transcendental attributes of Being, because they surpass all the limits of essences and are co-extensive with Being. If there is an insurmountable distance between God and his creature, but if there is also an analogy between them that cannot be resolved in any form of identity, there must also exist an analogy between the transcendentals—between those of the creature and those in God.

There are two conclusions to draw from this: one positive, the other negative. The positive: man exists only by interpersonal dialogue: therefore by language, speech (in gestures, in mimic or in words). Why then deny speech to Being himself? "In the beginning was the Word, and the Word was with God, and the Word was God" (John 1:1).

The negative: supposing that God is truly God (that is to say, that he is the totality of Being who has need of no creature), then God will be the plenitude of the One, the good, the True and the Beautiful, and by consequence the limited creature participates in the transcendentals only in a partial, fragmentary fashion. Let us take an example: What is unity in a finite world? Is it the species (each man is totally man, *that* is his unity), or is it the individual (each man is indivisibly himself)? Unity is thus polarized in the domain of finitude. One can demonstrate the same polarity for the Good, the True and the Beautiful.

I have thus tried to construct a philosophy and a theology starting from an analogy, not of an abstract Being, but of Being as it is encountered concretely in its attributes (not categorical, but transcendental). And as the transcendentals run through all Being, they must be interior to each other: that which is truly true is also truly good and beautiful and one. A being *appears*, it has an epiphany: in that it is beautiful and makes us marvel. In appearing it *gives* itself, it delivers itself to us: it is good. And in giving itself up, it *speaks* itself, it unveils itself: it is true (in itself, but in the other to which it reveals itself).

Thus one can construct above all a theological *Ästhetik* (*Herrlichkeit*):[1] God appears. He appeared to Abraham, to Moses, to Isaiah, finally in Jesus Christ. A theological question: How do we distinguish his appearance, his epiphany, among the thousand other phenomena in the world? How do we distinguish the true and only living God of Israel from all the idols that surround him and from all the philosophical and theological attempts to attain God? How do we perceive the incomparable glory of God in the life, the Cross, the Resurrection

---

[1] *Herrlichkeit. Eine theologische Ästhetik* (Einsiedeln, Johannes Verlag) vol. 1: *Schau der Gestalt* (1961; 3d ed., 1988); vol. 2: *Fächer der Stile*; part 1: *Klerikale Stile* (1962; 3d ed., 1984); part 2: *Laikale Stile* (1962; 3d ed., 1984); vol. 3/1: *Im Raum der Metaphysik*; part 1: *Altertum* (1965; 2d ed., 1975); part 2: *Neuzeit* (1965; 2d ed., 1975); vol. 3/2: *Theologie*; part 1: *Alter Bund* (1966; 2d ed., 1989); part 2: *Neuer Bund* (1969; 2d ed., 1988).

English translation: *The Glory of the Lord: A Theological Aesthetics* (vols. 1–2: San Francisco: Ignatius Press, New York: Crossroad; vols. 3–7: San Francisco, Ignatius Press). Vol. 1: *Seeing the Form* (1982); vol. 2: *Studies in Theological Style: Clerical Styles* (1984); vol. 3: *Studies in Theological Style: Lay Styles* (1986); vol. 4: *The Realm of Metaphysics in Antiquity* (1989); vol. 5: *The Realm of Metaphysics in the Modern Age* (1991); vol. 6: *Theology: The Old Covenant* (1991); vol. 7: *Theology: The New Covenant* (1989).

of Christ, a glory different from all other glory in this world?

One can then continue with a *Dramatik*,[2] since this God enters into an alliance with us: How does the absolute liberty of God in Jesus Christ confront the relative, but true, liberty of man? Will there perhaps be a mortal struggle between the two in which each one will defend against the other what it conceives and chooses as the good? What will be the unfolding of the battle, the final victory?

One can conclude with a *Logik* (*Theo-logik*).[3] How can God come to make himself understood to man, how can an infinite Word express itself in a finite word without losing its sense? That will be the problem of the two natures of Jesus Christ. And how can the limited spirit of man come to grasp the unlimited sense of the Word of God? That will be the problem of the Holy Spirit.

This, then, is the articulation of my trilogy. I have meant only to mention the questions posed by the method, without coming to the responses, because that would go well beyond the limits of an introductory summary such as this.

---

[2] *Theodramatik* (Einsiedeln, Johannes Verlag) vol. 1: *Prolegomena* (1973); vol. 2: *Die Personen des Spiels*; part 1: *Der Mensch in Gott* (1976); part 2: *Die Personen in Christus* (1978); vol. 3: *Die Handlung* (1980); vol. 4: *Das Endspiel* (1983).

English translation: *Theo-Drama: Theological Dramatic Theory* (San Francisco, Ignatius Press). Vol. 1: *Prolegomena* (1988); vol. 2: *Dramatis Personae: Man in God* (1990); vol. 3: *Dramatis Personae: Persons in Christ* (1992); vol. 4: *The Action* (1993); vol. 5: *The Last Act* (in preparation).

[3] *Theologik* (Einsiedeln, Johannes Verlag) vol. 1: *Wahrheit der Welt* (1985); vol. 2: *Wahrheit Gottes* (1985); vol. 3: *Der Geist der Wahrheit* (1987). English translation in preparation.

In conclusion, it is nonetheless necessary to touch briefly on the Christian response to the question posed in the beginning relative to the religious philosophies of humanity. I say the Christian response, because the responses of the Old Testament and a fortiori of Islam (which remains essentially in the enclosure of the religion of Israel) are incapable of giving a satisfactory answer to the question of why Yahweh, why Allah, created a world of which he did not have need in order to be God. Only the fact is affirmed in the two religions, not the why.

The Christian response is contained in these two fundamental dogmas: that of the Trinity and that of the Incarnation. In the trinitarian dogma, God is one, good, true and beautiful because he is essentially Love, and Love supposes the one, the other and their unity. And if it is necessary to suppose the Other, the Word, the Son, in God, then the otherness of the creation is not a fall, a disgrace, but an image of God, even as it is not God.

And as the Son in God is the eternal icon of the Father, he can without contradiction assume in himself the image that is the creation, purify it and make it enter into the communion of the divine life without dissolving it (in a false mysticism). It is here that one must distinguish nature and grace.

All true solutions offered by the Christian Faith hold, therefore, to these two mysteries, categorically refused by a human reason that makes itself that absolute. It is because of this that the true battle between religions begins only after the coming of Christ. Humanity will prefer to renounce all philosophical questions—in Marxism, or positivism of all stripes, rather than accept a philosophy that finds its final response only in the revelation of Christ.

Foreseeing that, Christ sent his believers into the whole world as sheep among wolves.

Before making a pact with the world, it is necessary to meditate on that comparison.

INDEX OF PERSONS